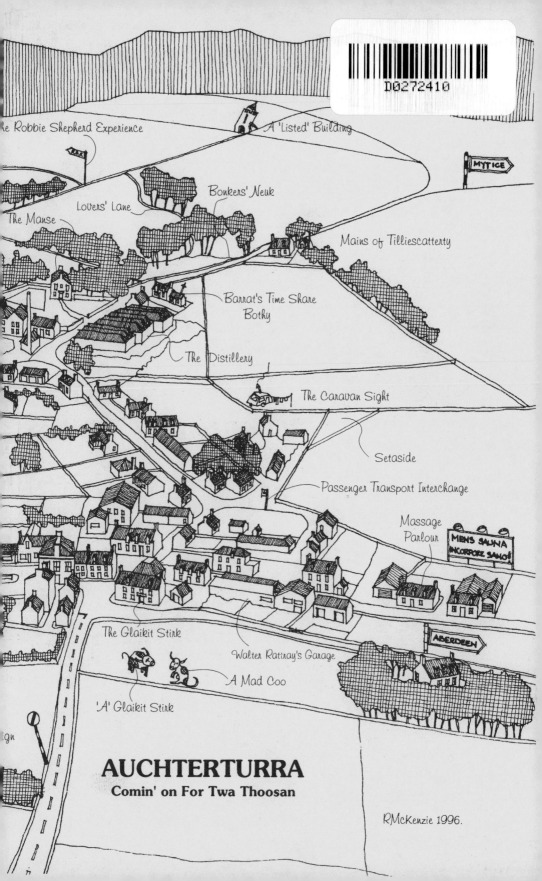

The Robbie Shepherd Experience

A 'Listed' Building

MYTICE

Bonkers' Neuk

Lovers' Lane

The Manse

Mains of Tilliescatterty

Barrat's Time Share Bothy

The Distillery

The Caravan Sight

Setaside

Passenger Transport Interchange

Massage Parlour

MENS SAUNA INCORPORE SANO!

The Glaikit Stirk

Walter Rattray's Garage

ABERDEEN

A Mad Coo

'A' Glaikit Stirk

AUCHTERTURRA
Comin' on For Twa Thoosan

R McKenzie 1996.

SCOTLAND THE WHAT?
Second Helping

BY THE SAME AUTHORS

Scotland the What? Gordon Wright Publishing 1987.

SCOTLAND THE WHAT?
Second Helping

Written by
BUFF HARDIE and STEPHEN ROBERTSON

Music by
GEORGE DONALD

Lyrics by
BUFF HARDIE

Directed for the Stage by
JAMES LOGAN
and
ALAN FRANCHI

GORDON WRIGHT PUBLISHING
25 MAYFIELD ROAD, EDINBURGH EH9 2NQ
SCOTLAND

British Library Cataloguing in Publication Data
A Catalogue for this book is available
from the British Library.

ISBN 0 903065 85 1

PHOTO CREDITS. Page numbers given.
Gordon Wright: 14 top, 17 top, 19 top/r, 38, 46, 82, 88, 100, 112, 133, 144, 149, 151, 160, 163, 173, 185, 236, 241, 260, 268, 277.
Grampian Television: Front cover, Back cover, 14 bot., 15 bot., 16 top, 69, 97, 124, 170, 216, 227, 230.
Aberdeen Journals Ltd.: 19 top/l, 20 bot., 80, 146, 198, 271, 273.
Donald Stewart: 20 top, 140, 180, 286.
Doug Westland: 22, 31, 47, 67.
Aberdeen District Council: 16 bot.
Jim Henderson: 19 bot.
Louis Flood: 29.
B.B.C.: 15 top, 84.
Grampian Police: 142.
D C Thomson & Co Ltd.: 159.
Alan Franchi: 251.
STW?: 18 top.

Peter Garland: Computer generated musical notation.
Roddy McKenzie: Maps of Auchterturra.
Sandy Cheyne: Cartoons.

Typeset by Gordon Wright Publishing Ltd., Edinburgh.
Printed and Bound by Redwood Books, Trowbridge.

Contents

Prologue . . . and Epilogue 9

'Six Cripplers and Nae Holies' 11

A Few Snaps from the Scrap-Book 14

1988

Trans-Buchan Airways 21

Video Man 24

In the Garden 30

Towards 2000 36

Doctors' Reunion 38

The Session Clerk 45

A Heart-Beat Away 48

The Hundred Fiddlers 51

Doctor and Patient 55

The Bottle Bank 58

King James 60

The Ozone Layer 62

The Indian Restaurateur 65

Life's not Easy 70

The Fish Farmer 73

The Prince of Wales 75

City of Culture 76

Mastermind 81

Neighbours 85

Election '99 87

Lord Chancellor's Song   91

Headlines 1988   93

1991

Three Tenors   94

The M.O.T. Test   101

The Edinburgh Smell   104

Nona's Knickers   108

I Know the Face   110

The Census   116

How About You?   121

School Chums   123

Junk Mail   130

The Insurance Policy   132

Proud to be Scottish   137

Police News   141

Nicky Tams   147

The New MP   150

Dinosaurs   152

Auchterturra TV: Late Call   155

Plastic Card   156

Big Nose   160

Taxi Driver   163

You're Here   168

1992

The Christening   171

Columbus   174

At the Palace   180

Silver Lining   184

Dod 'n' Bunty   186

Rave-up at Rhynie   190

Morning Coffee   192

I've Seen the Day   195

The Operation   199

Hogmanay in Auchterturra   205

1995

Councillor Swick   232

The Holiday Maker   235

You're the Top   239

Grandad's Birthday   240

The Diet Starts Tomorrow   245

Press Conference   250

Talking Britain Down   255

The Mascot   260

The Fund-Raiser   265

Peter Snow   270

The Way it Was   272

Retirement   277

We Are Failing   285

Fittie Folk   287

Prologue . . .

Prologue? Well, William Shakespeare and Ernie Wise both had prologues to the plays what they wrote and what better precedents to follow? Class acts both, although historical records show that Anne Hathaway wasn't quite as funny as Eric Morecambe. And although what follows isn't a play it does aspire to be a serious reproduction of a theatrical entertainment. So why *not* prologue . . . ?

'Gosh, doesn't time fly?' as Lord Byron once said (to continue the literary theme) with that clarity of vision and mastery of language which made him Aberdeen Grammar School's most famous F. P. – i.e. Former Pupil – nae jist Famous Poet. Well, yes it does. It is nine years since the publication of Scotland The What?'s last book – last, first and only, until now. Nine flying years – flying and vanishing with a swiftness that implies an extremely serious chronological challenge; flying about the country from Shetland to Kirkcudbright, Oban to St. Andrews and three score venues and ten in between – from village hall to school platform and Scout Hut, to mention only the more glamorous engagements; flying the flag of passé revue cum couthy concert which kind of sums up what we did in S.T.W.? for more than twenty-six years, not just nine. Twenty-six years in dinner jackets and black ties trying to squeeze a laugh out of the sceptical Scottish bourgeoisie, themselves a *collective* chronological challenge. We remember the night at Pitlochry a few years ago when we started the show and thought there were teething troubles with a new sound system. Was that the reason for the series of high-pitched whistling noises in the first five minutes? 'Oh no,' said the resident stage manager, 'that's just everybody switching on their hearing aids.' Right enough. As we took turns to look through the peephole in the side curtain – a magnet for the performer of masochistic tendencies, we scanned a sea of elderly respectability, glinting spectacles, blue rinses and balding pates. In self-defence Pitlochry is seething with holiday geriatrics anyway – they hadn't *all* gathered at the Festival Theatre to see Scotland The What? And not all pillars of the bourgeoisie are senior citizens – there are slightly younger elements. Like ourselves. When we first went to the Edinburgh Festival Fringe in 1969 Allen Wright of *The Scotsman* wrote ' . . . bourgeois and proud of it! A lawyer, a teacher and a civil servant from Aberdeen, they have strolled into the Fringe and caused an uproar of laughter. By revue standards they are elderly (they must be at least thirty) and they are sedately dressed in dinner jackets.'

During the quarter of a century which followed we came to identify even more closely with our audiences and took the view that they were not only 'middle-aged, middle-brow, middle-class' but also intelligent, demanding and, happily for us, still continuing to share the same terms of reference and sense of humour. Quite discriminating people really – but only *quite* discriminating, not *really* discriminating. Which probably also means *you*, dear reader, or the opinion of you held by whoever made you a gift of this book – because it's unlikely you would have bought it yourself if you were *really* discriminating . . .

. . . and Epilogue

Epilogue? Right after the Prologue? Yes, because this book is itself an epilogue. It follows our last stage show which we called 'Final Fling' and lets us say something about it.

It was early 1994 when the truth dawned that we were all pushing sixty – backwards. The hurly-burly of the theatre circuit and the need to change the material for every engagement were getting irksome so we decided to celebrate our Silver Anniversary due in September that year with the announcement of a Farewell Tour. Not so much a tour perhaps as a series of visits for a last curtain-call at all the places we had appeared or as many of them as were prepared to have us back. Happily most were, and so 'Final Fling' and the Farewell Tour took shape, the key booking being His Majesty's, Aberdeen, where we wanted to finish and where to our great satisfaction our last season was also the last booking made before his retiral by Jimmy Donald the Director, who had been such a good friend to us from the beginning. Everything else then fell gradually into place and so between October 1994 and November 1995 we stravaiged the country visiting old haunts and watering-holes and winkling fellow couch-potatoes away from their tellies for a last rendezvous over the footlights with the inhabitants and idiosyncrasies of Auchterturra. Away from the footlights we found ourselves at the receiving-end of some wonderful hospitality. One of the nice things about doing S.T.W.? was always the emergence of old friends and these appeared in droves during that last year. 'Bliss was it in that social twilight to be alive but to be retiring was very heaven' as Bill Wordsworth would have said had he been lucky enough to be with us. We felt very spoiled and were glad to reciprocate when we reached home, throwing a series of parties for our out-of-town guests. Our last night at His Majesty's on 25 November 1995 was, of course, particularly special and we had to restrict the guest-list for the after-show party that night to immediate helpers and the S.T.W.? extended family. Because behind the scenes S.T.W.? has been very much a family affair – the families have always been close friends, the most momentous personal event in the whole S.T.W.? story being the sad loss of James Logan in November 1993 (see p.11). However, sticking to the bright side we report with pleasure that the S.T.W.? families have since publication of the last book had seven weddings, nine grand-children (including one lot of twins) and not a single divorce – so we're as bourgeois and proud of it as we were back in 1969. By a happy coincidence too, our prolonged leave-taking, the official end of a long and most enjoyable innings, was marked by a kind of official acceptance. In November 1994 Aberdeen University where we first met and where all this nonsense really began, gave us honorary degrees and in December 1995 just after the Farewell Tour we made the trip to Buckingham Palace to receive gongs from Her Majesty. Good Heavens! Welcomed by both the academic aristocracy and by Royalty itself! But what about that sceptical bourgeoisie? We suspect that they also *may* have given us the seal of approval by this time. Mind you, the approval would be of a kind which is only *quite,* not *really* discriminating.

Stephen Robertson.

'Six Cripplers and Nae Holies.'

'I dust the piano, and on bad nights sell the ice-cream,' was how James Logan was wont to describe his contribution to *Scotland the What?* Which was nonsense, of course. He never sold ice-cream. But I do have memories of him dusting the piano, slowly and carefully, at a late stage in the preparation for a performance, his rationale being, as he once explained, that having given up on the performers' appearance, he could at least make the piano look immaculate.

His death in 1993 deprived us not only of a superb duster of pianos, but also of a director, script editor, agent, road manager, publicity officer and, most of all, friend. While trying to create laughter in a theatre is a serious business, or at least a business to be taken seriously – and over the years there were anxious moments and minor crises – the whole *Scotland the What?* operation, which after all had begun as an enjoyable hobby, never stopped being great fun, to which James's was always a major contribution. He could generate laughter on any occasion whether with the spontaneous one-liner or the big set-piece anecdote.

The finely-honed dramatised comic anecdote found him at his best. It was a best, however, which he tended to fall short of when he was telling a story more mundane in character and not requiring the economy of a tight theatrical narrative. In these circumstances he could get a little bogged down in details not immediately germane to his purpose. Years ago, before we all gave up the day jobs, we had a rehearsal problem through the week with George living in Perth and the rest of us in Aberdeen. We managed to even out the travelling by obtaining the permission of the Rev Peter Gordon, the then minister of Brechin Cathedral, and himself an Aberdeen Student Show alumnus, to rehearse in the Cathedral hall. Following a rigorous two-hour session, we would adjourn for a half-pint before making our separate ways home, and some nights we would enjoy an al fresco supper purchased from the Savoy Fish and Chip Shop. Service in the Savoy was never lightning-fast, and one evening when George was inside the shop obtaining the suppers, the rest of us stayed in the car where after some time we were approached by a policeman who enquired as to our business. Assuming the role of spokesman, James said, 'My name is James Logan, I am a research chemist at the Macaulay Institute for Soil Research in Aberdeen. My two colleagues are Mr Robertson, who is a solicitor in Aberdeen, and Mr Hardie, who is the Secretary of the Grampian Health Board. We are waiting for our friend Mr George Donald, the Assistant Rector of Perth Academy, who is in the chip shop for two white pudding suppers and two haddock suppers, because since eight o'clock this evening we've been singing comic songs in Brechin Cathedral.' 'Oh, you're *Scotland the What?*' said the bobby. 'You should have said.'

But to return to James's skill as a comic raconteur, this was born of his gift for the theatrical, which in turn made him a sharply perceptive and ruthless script editor, saving many a *Scotland the What?* sketch from the authors' self-indulgence, always to the benefit of the show and with the incidental result in the present context of ensuring that the sketches published in this book are to be found at their fighting weight. Once an idea had found favour and seemed worthy of development, James would say, 'Six cripplers – that's all you need, lads.' In his direction of the show his prime objective was always that nothing should get in the way of the material, and his aim was that the presentation should be sharp, focussed, unfussy, pacey and with 'nae holies', that is to say, no moments, however short, during which the audience was not totally engaged.

As to the direction of dialogue, except in the very occasional case, he sensibly took the view that there was little point in telling the writers how to say their own lines, but there were certain instructions which he did have for us: visiting the dressing-room just before curtain up with 'A small refreshment, Sir Stephen?' he would enjoin us to 'fizz', and ask us for 'a little *joie*, this evening.' reserving for me the exhortation, 'Never mind if the *Sunday Post* called you a deadpan comic, you can still muster a bit of *joie*.' He was in no doubt that *joie* held the key. One night when a number of things had gone wrong, we came off bemoaning our errors, but James greeted us with, 'Mistakes? Totally minor. The *joie* was great.'

Joie was what the theatre brought to him. He loved sitting as a member of an audience in a darkened theatre waiting to be surprised. And he loved being part of the panoply and ritual of the theatre – in however humble a capacity. 'Ticket-holders only, this way,' we could hear him say in his capacity as chief usher on the last night of our first venture on the Edinburgh Festival Fringe in 1969, when, against all our wildest expectations, the 280-seater St Mary's Cathedral Hall was full. 'And it's the carriage trade to-night,' he reported to us later, 'lang frocks an a' thing.' The piano had been well-dusted that night.

James knew the words of all the songs and all the sketches in the show. And if any of the performers ever felt slightly under the weather, there could be no stronger incentive to buckle to, get out there and make with the show-must-go-on spirit than the thought that James was ready to understudy. He never did get a spot in the show to himself. I grieve enormously that he has had this spot to himself in this book.

Buff Hardie.

James Logan

A few snaps from the scrap-book . . .

Dressing for afternoon tea has always been a feature of our rigorous rehearsal schedule.

But it has not all been hard work: life with Scotland the What? has given us opportunities to meet many interesting people; like Ricky Demarco . . .

... and fellow performers from the BBC's *Halls of Fame* from His Majesty's Theatre, Aberdeen
. . .

... and the eponymous presenter of Grampian TV's Art Sutter Show ...

. . . and the (exceedingly) retiring chief executive of Grampian TV, Alec Mair, whom we
auditioned at his farewell do as a potential Rawicz to George's Landauer . . .

. . . and also some really important people such as Aberdeen's first female Lord Provost,
Cllr. Margaret Farquhar . . .

16

. . . and even more important, our genial Edinburgh publisher and notable dumpling-maker, Gordon 'Clootie' Wright . . .

. . . and most important of all, our fans, or some of them (most of them?).

Some unexpected, but very gratifying honours have come our way: the MBE, conferred by the Queen at Buckingham Palace . . .

. . . and the honorary degree of Master of the University from Aberdeen University where it all began. This post-ceremony group includes our old friend Jimmy Donald, former manager of His Majesty's Theatre, who received the same honour, and University Principal, Prof. Maxwell Irvine (centre).

They also serve: the 'indispensable rock on which the sometimes teetering edifice of Scotland the What? has leant,' business manager, Graham Hunter.

Alan Franchi, director of our television shows, but despite that experience, persuaded to take over from James as director of our stage shows.

With the backstage team, without whom our farewell tour and Final Fling would never have happened: L to R: Peter Garland our long-time stage manager; Alan Franchi our Director; and sound wizard David Eastwood.

25 November 1995 and Peter waits in the prompt corner at His Majesty's as the clock shows 7.30pm. Time for the curtain to rise on the very last theatre performance of Scotland the What? which is preceded, as every performance has been since 1969, by the ritual handshakes.

And finally . . . ever encouraging, constructively critical, staunchly supportive, and nice with it, the Scotland the What? wives photographed together in 1992. L to R: Anne Logan, Eva Robertson, Isabelle Donald and Margaret Hardie.

Trans-Buchan Airways

A pilot (Steve) is discovered seated at the controls of an aircraft. He addresses the passengers.

Good morning, ladies and gentlemen . . . Trans-Buchan Airways welcomes you aboard their breakfast time shuttle from Ellon to Huntly. Flight number TBA clickety-click, dinky-doos, unlucky for some.

This is your captain spikkin, Captain Davie 'Biggles' Henderson, and I hope that you have a very pleasant flight. Our scheduled take-off time this morning is 08.00 hours, so wi a bit o luck we should be roaded by half ten. On behalf of Trans-Buchan Airways I apologise for the delay but one of our passengers this mornin is a coo gaan tae the mart, and the security lads hid an affa job gettin her through the X-Ray machine. An God, ye'll nivver believe this. Fan they saw the X-Ray plates there wis a touchie brucellosis showed up. So that's the wye we noo hiv a coo in quarantine in the toilet, at the hinner end o the plane. So if ony o ye is wintin tae ging tae the bathroom ye'd better get aff an ging noo. Cos aat's yer last chance afore the Square at Huntly.

Now our cruising speed this morning will be sixty mile an oor. Aye, nae aa the time. And our arrival time at Huntly will be 11.25 hours. That is not, repeat not, an estimate – it's a complete shot in the dark. We will be flying at a height of 1701 feet 6 inches, which is a good three feet higher than the Mither Tap on Bennachie. So we should clear it easy enough. Weel, pit it iss wye, we've nivver hit it yet.

Now, afore I ging ony further I'd better get the bad news oot o the wye. We hinna got a navigator the day. As a matter o fact he's jist been on the phone sayin he's hid tae ging doon tae Forfar tae pick up his new guide dog. He's nae sure if he's gettin an Airedale or a Skye Terrier. So aat's the bad news. The good news is – we've got a much better chance o gettin there withoot im.

Now Trans-Buchan Airways is reid hot on safety. So first of all here's the drill for fit tae dee if we come doon in the sea. Now, gaan fae Ellon tae Huntly we shouldna come doon in the sea, especially the day fin we hinna got the handicap o a navigator. But jist in case we div come doon in the sea there's a bit o drill wi yer life jecket, an I'll jist read it oot tae ye.

Right now! Step 1. Locate aperture in life jacket and insert head. – Rug the jecket ower yer heid through the holie in the tap.

Step 2: Feed the white cord under each armpit. – Pull the white tow aneth baith yer oxters.

Step 3: Stretch the cord around the abdomen carefully in order to avoid discomfort.

– Caa the tow roon yer belly an dinna rax yersel.

Now, this next announcement is for those passengers with seatbelts. Wid ye please baith fasten them. On this flight the passengers with the seatbelts are the occupants of seats A7 and B14, 'cos they were the winners o the lucky draa.

Runner-up in the lucky draa is the occupant of seat D9 and his prize is first shottie o the sick bag. As you were . . . second shottie . . . I'm jist gettin the message comin through . . . the coo's been sick aaready.

Now this aircraft is jist aboot ready tae tik aff. Jist as seen as we get the frost scraped aff the windscreen. Thank God it's July. During take-off I would advise you to sit well back in your seat, shut yer een, cross yer fingers and hope like hell. 'Cos by God aat's fit I'm gaan tae be deein. Right now . . . (*Sound of engine starting*) Contact . . . chocks away . . . and suck yer barley sugars instead.

Oh, my God, aat wiz a hairy een. Faar the hell did that silo come fae? Oh, they should tell ye aboot things like that. Nivver mind we're here, we're here, we're up first shottie the day. Last Tuesday we hid tae get the jump leads on til't.

Now instead of the usual inflight movie, we've got a special treat for ye the day – I'm gaan tae pass roon my holiday snaps. Me an the wife went on a SAGA bus tour last summer . . . an we got affa pally wi the driver. Fit a fine lad. An ye ken, he drove twaa hunner miles wi sixty-three passengers on his bus. I jist couldna cope wi that kind o responsibility.

Oh, there's anither interesting sight . . . now that is a right landmark there, now that's Mormond Hill an it's jist bristlin wi NATO defence equipment. God, there's radar an scanners an satellite dishes, aa the dirt o the day, fit a battery o stuff there is. I'll jist tak the plane a wee bitty closer so ye can hae a better look . . . (*Sound of rockets*) . . . God aat's rockets they're firing the day . . . some days it's shells . . . (*Sound of shell*) . . . God aat's shells an aa the day. It's nae every day ye get rockets an shells the same day, bit dinna worry aboot it, there's no danger ladies and gentlemen, no danger at all. They're aa fired by computer, and the computer jist canna comprehend that there's ony plane could fly as low, or as slow, as Trans-Buchan Airways.

Brucellosis: Bovine disease named after King Robert the Bruce (1274-1329) who contracted it during one of his visits to the North-East when he took part in a Buchan Bronco competition at the Cairnbulg Stampede. (1316, or possibly 1317 – historians disagree.)

Square at Huntly: Note this piece of dramatic licence. In fact there are no public conveniences in the Square at Huntly, but no matter, anywhere in Huntly you're never far from the woods and the fields.

Usual in-flight movie: *One of our Aircraft is Missing* (1942) withdrawn by public demand.

Video Man

ne - ver have ti - me to watch them. Charles and Di - an - a's

wed - ding day I've got that on tape.

Scotch and Wry on Hog - man - ay I've got that on

tape. 'Yes Prime Min - is - ter' that was tre - men - dous.

Ev' - ry cri - sis there's been on East - end -ers. Ev' ry Wog -an since it ev - er

start - ed and the night Hil - da Og - don de - part - ed Ev' - ry

tal - ent - ed tel - e - vis - ion per - son Not just them, al - so Ar - chie Mac-

pher - son. My Wife has a grouse 'Cos my tapes fill the house But I

ne - ver have time to watch them.

Coda

But I'm not so

cle - ver be - cause I don't ev - er I nev - er have time to

watch them.

If, like me, you're a devotee
Of ev'rything that is on TV,
A video recorder just has to be
An absolute necessity.
I've got programmes taped by the score,
I take care I never botch them,
But the thing that makes me sore
Is I can't find the time to watch them –

Charles and Diana's wedding day
– I've got that on tape
Scotch and Wry on Hogmanay
– I've got that on tape
Yes, Prime Minister – that was tremendous –
Ev'ry crisis there's been on *Eastenders*;
Ev'ry *Wogan* since it ever started
And the night Hilda Ogden departed;
Ev'ry talented television person –
Not just them, also Archie McPherson.
My wife has a grouse,
'Cos my tapes fill the house,
And I never have time to watch them.

Every snooker shot Stephen Hendry has played –
I've got them on tape.
The Queen's horse fertilising all Horse Guard's Parade –
I've got that on tape.
And my favourite, *Living and Growing,*
Fifteenth series and twentieth showing.
Ronald Reagan who, though getting on, is
The funniest by far of the Ronnies.
And baseball: the Bears v the Yankees;
Melvyn Bragg interviewing the Crankies.
Oh, you can't get a drink
For the tapes in the sink
But I never have time to watch them.

Three times a week, *Coronation Street* –
I've got that on tape.
Frank Gilfeather – whoops – falling off the seat –
I've got that on tape.
Louis Armstrong, the daddy of jazz, or
Jimmy Hill going nuts over Gazza.
I've taped, with amazing perversity –
The whole of the Open University.
Pavarotti 'n' his two chums – a great show
Rab C Nesbitt discussed on the Late Show.
I've got tapes by the crate
But I guess it's my fate
To never have time to watch them.

Horowicz performing a Polonaise
– I've got that on tape.
Judith Chalmers enjoying some free holidays
– I've got that on tape.
Programmes British and programmes American,
Michael Fish saying, 'There won't be a Hurricane'.
Joan Collins – a great acress, isn't she?
In that show that my Grannie called '*Dysentery*'.
The Queen Mum having a dram on her birthday
Well, at ninety you get very thirthday!
My collection's so large
That I've filled the garage;
Tapes of every sort
But life is too short –
I never have time to watch them.

The marvellous *Jewel in the Crown* –
I've got that on tape.
Jer'my Beadle bringing the standards back down –
I've got that on tape.
Ian Botham in the footsteps of Hannibal
Causing bunions for some big dumb animal.
All the films Barry Norman thought sordid
You can bet your sweet life I've recorded.
Johnny Weissmuller yod'lling his mate call
Bernard Manning excelling on *Late Call*.
Our baby cries a lot
'Cos there's tapes in his cot,
But I'm not so clever
Because I don't ever –
I never have time to watch them.

In the Garden

Norman (Buff) is discovered holding a graip with a potato impaled on a prong.

N. Michty, I've murdered aat tattie.

Enter Alec (Steve)

A. Aye, aye, Norman.

N. God, if it's nae yersel, Alec. Ye're a stranger. Come in.

A. No, I'm nae comin in. I see ye're liftin yer tatties. I'll let ye get on.

N. Aye. I'll need tae get on. I'm liftin my Edzell Blues. I jist funcied chips for my denner. An Tibby says tae me, 'Weel, if ye're wintin chips, we'll need tatties.'

A. My God! She's a clever woman. Ye've got a topper there, boy. You can pick them, Norman.

N. So that's the wye I'm liftin tatties. 'Cos I like chips.

A. Weel, you are laughin boy. Aat een's jist aboot intae chips aaready. Weel, but I'll let ye get on. God is aat a bee? Is aat een o your bees?

N. Faar aboot?

A. Buzzin aboot. God! it's intae yer lupins. No he's oot o yer lupins. He's up tae the tap o yer windae there. And oh! he's roon the back o yer lum.

N. Oh, I jist saw the back o im. I never got a look at his face.

A. So ye dinna ken if he wis een o your bees?

N. I dinna think he wis. My bees took a terrible hammerin in the winter.

A. Oh, but it wis a bad winter for bees, Norman.

N. Oh, it wis a terrible winter for bees. Weel, I'll tell ye, I've only three bees left.

A. Three bees left?

N. Three bees left. I've aye got Jocky.

A. Jocky! Oh I'm affa pleased tae hear ye've aye got Jocky. Oh, fit a character, Jocky. Is he aye keepin as busy?

N. Aye, he's aye as busy. D'ye mind it wis Jocky that wis lost doon the front o Tibby's frock?

A. Aye, She'd a bee in her bosie.

N. It wis affa good o ye tae gie's a hand tae get im oot.

A. Oh, but I widna see ye stuck, Norman. It's jist a peety he cam oot sae quick.

N. Weel, aat's Jocky. And then I've aye got Willie.

A. Willie.

N. Peer Willie.

A. Aye. He's an affa dwaibly, peely-wally kind o billy, Willie.

N. Aat's richt. It's a wonder he cam through the winter.

A. I'm surprised he cam through the summer.

N. So I've got Jocky an Willie, an then I've got Jessie.

A. Jessie? Aat's an affa funny name for a bee – Jessie.

N. Weel, we caa im Jessie cause he is a bit o a Jessie. He's aa richt as lang as he's fleein an hummin, but as seen as he lands, he walks affa Jessie kind.

A. A Jessie walker?

N. I dinna ken his second name.

A. Weel, but onywye that explains it, Norman.

N. Explains fit?

A. Onytime I've seen im buzzin aboot yer gairden he aye seems tae be amon the pansies. Weel, but I'll let ye get on.

N. Aye, I'll need tae get on.

A.   I'll let ye get on. Oh, Norman, I forgot tae thank ye for yer holiday postcaird. Yon wis an affa bonny view. Faar wis't ye wis?

N.   Peterheid.

A.   Lovely. For yer hale fortnicht?

N.   No. Jist a day.

A.   Aat's even better.

N.   Tell me, did ye like the picter on the postcaird? Aat's far we hid wir picnic.

A.   God, Norman, I never kent ye could get as near the prison as that.

N.   Aye. We'd wir picnic richt up against the waa o the prison. It's the only place in Peterheid far ye're oot o the wind.

A.   So ye jist hid days here an there, hid ye?

N.   Days here an there, aat's richt. We'd a day in Mintlaw.

A.   God, ye didna dae Mintlaw in a day, did ye? That wis goin some.

N.   Then we'd a day in New Byth. We'd an ice-cream there.

A.   God, wis New Byth nae caal enough already for ye?

N.   No, we'd een o that big cones wi the chocolate stickin oot the tap.

A.   Each? That wis lashin oot, wisn't it, Norman?

N.   No. Nae each. Atween's. Atween's.

A.   Of course.

N.   Then we'd a mornin in Cairnbulg.

A.   That hid been a high spot.

N.   Aye. It wis a high spot, aat.

A.   Did ye ging tae New Pitsligo?

N. No. I jist thocht, efter Cairnbulg, New Pitsligo wid be an anti-climax.

A. Oh aye. There's jist naething in New Pitsligo at aa. Nae efter Cairnbulg.

N. Weel, aat's fit we thocht. So we jist went straight tae Turriff, and we'd a bar supper in the Commercial Hotel.

A. Oh, I believe they do you very well.

N. Oh, very well. Mind you, I could hiv deen wi some mair chips.

A. Oh? Skimpy wi the chips?

N. No, scampi wi the chips. And then we'd a mystery tour tae Cuminestown. We finished up in the cemetery there. I pit a flooer on Granny's grave.

A. Oh, fit a cheery holiday ye hid, Norman.

N. Aye, we packed in a lot.

A. God, if it hid been me, I'd hiv packed in the hale thing.

N. No, no. Then we hid a day in Aiberdeen.

A. The divil that ye are, Norman. And did ye enjoy that?

N. Nae a lot. Tibby went mad in Marks an Spincers.

A. Oh, but it's a rare place, Marks an Spincers. They're affa good at changin things for ye. I mind I eence bocht a pair o troosers there. Wore them tae my work for a wik. Took them back an they changed them.

N. Weel, I tried that an they widna let me.

A. Oh? Fit hid you bocht?

N. A cabbage.

A. Weel, but I'll let ye get on.

N. Aye. I'll need tae get on.

A. I'll let ye get on. Oh, now, I forgot tae say, did ye get my holiday postcaird? Aye, fae France.

N. Aye, I got it. Thanks very much, it wis affa good o ye.

A. Wis ye ever in France yersel, Norman?

N. Jist eence. It wis a lang time ago. Never again. It wis an affa squash in the boat comin back.

A. Oh? Faar did ye come back fae?

N. Dunkirk. Aye, look, this is the postcaird. I've got it here.

A. That's it. Ho, ho!

N. That's it, ye see. Now, ye see, Tibby wisna affa happy aboot the picter o the lassie wi nae claes on.

A. Oh Norman, I'm affa sorry aboot aat. Aat's the Folies Bergeres, aat. I'll ken nae tae send ye ony mair postcairds like aat.

N. Aat's richt. Dinna send them. Bring them hame an we'll look at them thegither. Fit are we standin here for, Alec? Come on in an hae a cup o tea.

A. No, I'm nae comin in – God, there's anither bee!

N. Oh, I saw that een's face. That *is* Jocky.

A. God, he's flown richt intae the hoose.

N. Oh, me! An Tibby's got on her flooery frock.

A. Oh, weel, I'd *better* come in.

I'm nae comin in: Scholars of the Scotland the What? canon, in particular of 'Arrival' (1986), will notice that Alec and Norman, *au fait* as ever with contemporary mores, are here indulging in role reversal.

Edzell Blues: True story. At one performance a friend sitting in the back row overheard her neighbour, a weather-beaten son of the soil, growl to his wife: 'That's never an Edzell Blue. I can see fae here it's a Kerr's Pink.'

Towards 2000

(Tune: Chariots of Fire)

Aal Scotland is cruisin
To a notable year,
Towards twaa thoosan –
It soon will be here.

And lots of new fashions
Ye can see creepin in,
As the twentieth siecle
Approaches its fin.

In Auchterturra on Deeside
We keep in step – we've got oor pride –
Like the rest o the country we're yuppified
In a kind of a way.

We're upwardly mobile
We'd nae be seen deid
Withoot a designer
Bunnet on wir heid
(In Auchterturra the day.)

It's een o yer fallacies
That we're fashion freaks;
We aa wear reid galluses
Tae hud up wir breeks.

And as the pub closes
The old cobbled streets
Resound tae the clatter
Of Gucci beets.
(In Auchterturra the day.)

In the pub the bar lunch
Is a culin'ry treat:
It's mince in the basket
They gie ye tae eat.
(In Auchterturra the day.)

Designer stubble –
We've got that by the ton;
It's nae on folk's faces –
It's aa ower the grun.

The lads' drinkin habits
Hiv altered this year –
It's now gin and tonic
They drink wi their beer.
(In Auchterturra the day.)

Of course you will get
The occasional chap
That loses the heid
And gings ower the tap.

For instance Dod Walker
The glaikit aal gype –
He's bocht a new tractor
Wi a blue rally stripe.

For Jimmy Tough let's say a few prayers:
'Insider dealin,' the fiscal declares,
'In Rhynie Manure Products shares,'
And they put him away.
(In Auchterturra the day.)

Noo each ootside watery
Has a foam-covered seat,
And every farm has a byre
With midden en suite.

Aiberdeenshire is now like the Isle of Dogs,
It's Burberries and Barbours that noo are wir togs;
And – wid ye believe it – there's twaa synagogues.
(In Auchterturra the day.)

Doctors' Reunion

A large hotel, the evening of a Medical Class Reunion. Henry (Buff) is discovered, glass in hand, reading the table plan. Enter Basil (Steve), drunk, singing 'The Good Ship Venus'.

B.   Hello, Henry, old boy.

H.   Basil! (*They shake hands, Basil shows Henry a ticket.*) There are two hundred doctors at this reunion and you're the drunkest. Takes some doing.

B.   Do you know when they're drawing the raffle?

H.   Basil, that's not a raffle ticket. That's your cloakroom ticket.

B.   Cloakroom ticket?

H.   Yes, it's quite a common system. After the dinner you take that ticket to the cloakroom and they'll give you a coat.

B.   Jolly good. I didn't have a coat when I came in.

H. I do enjoy coming up for this reunion. Far and away the highlight of my year.

B. God! You must have had a hellish year. Where is it you are? Newcastle?

H. Guildford.

B. I knew it was down there somewhere. Are you still in livers?

H. No.

B. Kidneys?

H. No. Hearts.

B. I knew it was something that wasn't on the menu tonight.

H. Can I get you another drink?

B. No. I'm going easy on the drink tonight.

H. Quite right. You're not to go over the score.

B. So I'm stopping at nineteen.

H. Remember last year, though? You and I – we got through some stuff.

B. We got through four gin and tonics.

H. Couple of bottles of white.

B. Couple of bottles of red.

H. The best part of a bottle of brandy.

B. To say nothing of the jug of beer.

H. And a bottle of port.

B. And after that lot – I hardly had room for the soup.

H. Isn't that Fred Marshall coming in?

B. Yes, that's Fred. Hello, Fred! (*thumping chest.*) How's the old – ? Keeping better? Much better? Jolly good. (*to Henry*) Looks bloody awful doesn't he?

H. Terrible. And isn't that Dougie McLeod?

B. Yes, that's Dougie. Hello, Dougie! (*thumping stomach*) How's the old – ? Keeping better? Much better? Jolly good. (*to Henry*) He looks even worse.

H. Here, who's that poor fellow with the terrible stoop?

B. That's my old friend, Graham Edwards.

H. Well did you know your friend Graham's got a thoracic kypho-scoliosis?

B. No, he's got an Alpha-Romeo.

H. No, no. Look how he's standing. That's a classic case of kypho-scoliosis of the spine.

B. I always thought he'd a bad back.

H. And do you see Jock Stanley there? Basil, why is Jock wearing that funny hat?

B. That's not a hat. That's his new wig.

H. Alopaecia?

B. Bless you.

H. Didn't he have a wig when he was a student?

B. Yes, a black one.

H. Ah, I get it. At his time of life now a black wig wouldn't be right.

B. Exactly. That's why he's wearing that red one.

H. Who's that Jock's speaking to? The poor chap with the stiff neck.

B. That's the chaplain to the University.

H. Oh, that's not a surgical collar?

B. No. It's a dog collar.

H. What's he doing at a medical reunion?

B. Well, we're all agnostics. We had to get somebody to say the grace.

H. Didn't he marry a girl in our year. Marjory Gray?

B. Did you hear the dreadful news about Marjory?

H. Marjory's not away?

B. Away with the milkman.

H. I'm so sorry for the Chaplain.

B. I'm even sorrier for the milkman. Here, you'll never guess who's just come out of the gents'.

H. Who?

B. Toady Troup.

H. Toady Troup?

B. Toady Troup.

H. How long has he been out?

B. He's just come out.

H. Not out of the gents, out of the jug. Over the limit wasn't he?

B. Over the Forth Road Bridge, damn near.

H. What did he get?

B. He got caught.

H. He's a survivor, though, old Toady. Wasn't he sitting beside you at last year's reunion?

B. Yes. Did you know Toady's got a glass eye now?

H. Did he tell you?

B. No. It came out in the conversation.

H. Quiet, Basil. He's looking this way.

B. Oh, no he isn't.

H.   Oh, look. Toady's cadging a drink off Victor Reid. I was speaking to Victor in the bar. He was telling me about the operation he had last month. Very nasty. My sister Muriel had the same.

B.   Muriel didn't have her prostate done? Oh, there's Jimmy. Hello, Jimmy! Oh, the eagles, they fly high . . . (*he sings; Henry joins in*).

H.   Easter tour, 1947.

B.   '48, wasn't it?

H.   '48.

B.   Jimmy was the skipper.

H.   Jimmy was the skipper. That's still the same kilt he's wearing. He should've stopped wearing that years ago.

B.   M'm. When he got his leg off.

H.   Aye, 'cos you can easily tell the tin one.

B.   Yes, they can never quite match the colour. You can't get that mottled effect artificially.

H.   And that's Dick Walker with him. Dick was the star of that tour. He was so athletic then.

B.   Yes, copes well with the zimmer, doesn't he?

H.   Then Dick went on to play scrum-half for Scotland.

B.   Damn fine player, Dick. Do you know, I once kept Dick out of the Varsity team?

H.   Were you a scrum-half?

B.   No, I was a selector. And I didn't like Dick's attitude to drink. He never touched a drop.

H.   Here, isn't that Sandy Middleton?

B.   That's Sandy.

H.   What news of Sandy?

B. Well, you won't believe this, but Sandy's been a bit off-colour.

H. No! What's up with Sandy?

B. It's one of those obscure things. Difficult to diagnose. And I can't remember the name.

H. Difficult name to remember?

B. Difficult name to remember.

H. Mumps?

B. No.

H. Flu?

B. No. It's a longer word than that.

H. A longer word?

B. In fact it's two words.

H. Two words?

B. Two medical words.

H. Ingrowing toe-nail?

B. No. I would have recognised an ingrowing toe-nail.

H. Runny nose?

B. That's it. Sandy's got a runny nose.

H. So that's Sandy. Who all have I seen tonight? Because Elizabeth will want to know when I get home. That's Sandy. And there was Fred. And Dougie. And your chum Graham. And Jock Stanley. And Toady Troup. And Jimmy One-Leg. You see, Elizabeth knew all these chaps.

B. And she'll be so pleased to hear they're all keeping so fit.

H. A lot fitter than I am. Some days I feel terrible. Very worrying at my age.

B. Nonsense, Henry. You'll live till you're sixty-five.

H. I am sixty-five.

B. What did I tell you? That'll be 15 guineas, please.

H. Money, money! That's all you chaps in general practice think about these days.

B. But I'm not in general practice any more. I've got a new job. And I'm enjoying it thoroughly.

H. What are you in now?

B. I'm in Health Education. (*exhales smoke and takes a drink from his glass.*)

Thoracic kypho-scoliosis: The authors wish to thank Dr Murdoch Shirreffs, Aberdeen, for telling them what an Alfa-Romeo is.

Glass eye: Basil must own a copy of a war-time 78 gramophone record of Vic Oliver entertaining the forces, in which this joke occurs. Where Vic Oliver pinched it from is not known.

General practice: When this sketch was revived for a cabaret we did for the Spring Symposium of the Royal College of General Practice (RCGP) we were pleased to discover that these initials can also be construed as standing for 'really convivial and genially plootered.'

The Session Clerk

The Session Clerk (Buff) ushers an unseen minister into an unseen seat.

Come away in, Mr McPherson, Reverend Sir. Sit you down there. It's a great pleasure for me as Session Clerk to welcome you here as our sole nominee for the joint charge of Boddam and Gomorrah.

You were the Assistant Minister at Crathie? What were your main duties? Car park attendant. And you had the concession for the postcards. Oh, well, you'd done aaricht, and your television fees an aa. Eh? You've never been on television? Never even been on *Reflections*? I thocht aa you boys got a shottie on *Reflections*. In fact I thocht onybody could get a shottie on *Reflections*. They've had an electrician that's seen the light; a gas engineer that's been converted; and a telephone operator that's answered the call. But you've never been on. Fit? Och, you could easy manage it. It used to be five minutes, but its only thirty-five seconds now. Includin a Jack Wilson commercial in the middle, which reminds me, how long is your sermons? Aye, on average. Well, ten minutes at the very ootside. You'll easy ken. Jist keep yer eye on Jessie Mackenzie in the second row fae the front: you've over-stepped the mark if she gets onto her third pandrop. An as lang as I mind, jist a wee word aboot the weekly service. We would like to have it on a Sunday. If that's OK wi you. I mean you're nae a golfer, are ye? No, the thing is the boy we had afore you wis a terrific golfer. He played aff scratch. An it didna suit him at aa tae hae the service on a Sunday. An he wanted to change it tae Thursday. Well, that would have suited me fine. But in a little place like this there's a lot o die-hards in the congregation – affa narrow folk, bigoted really, so fortunately for the survival of Christianity in Boddam he got a call to England. Aye, he's the pro at Sunningdale now.

So, Sunday's aaricht for you? That's fine. Now, hymns. We ken twelve hymns here. We ken 'All People', 'And Did Those Feet', 'Holy, Holy', 'Gladsome Mind', but I'll provide you with a comprehensive list of the twelve hymns that we ken and you can perm ony three oot o that twelve.

Now jist a word aboot the hatched, matched and despatched, which will of course constipate the main part of your duties here. Now christenings. For ony sake caa canny wi that bairns. The last mannie we had here it was like launchin a boat. Well Davy Duncan, the butcher, his loon's twelve-year-aal last birthday and he's still got web feet. Weddings, now all wedding receptions take place in the Gomorrah Arms, and very friendly gatherings they are, and we hope that you and your good lady will come along. Now do you tak a drink? That's fine, and dinna imagine for one moment that your ministerial calling exempts you from buyin a round. Funerals? Well that pits in mind o this: how long before you can take up duty? Well two weeks at the very ootside. I'll tell ye fit it is – aal Jimmy Gillanders, the saddler, he's ninety-eight, he's nae great but he's agreed to hing on as an obligement till you get here.

Noo this is nae the place for me tae ask ye onything aboot theology because I dinna ken onything aboot that kind of thing, and we dinna expect you to waste your time on't. But can ye say the Books o the Bible? Ye ken, Genesis, Exodus, Leviticus . . . Aff ye go then. Aye, aye . . . . Revelations. You passed on two, Obadiah and First Corinthians. Noo funcy nae gettin First Corinthians. Especially fan you got Second Corinthians. I mean, did ye nae realise that if there wis a Second Corinthians there wis a pretty fair chance there wis a First Corinthians? Never mind, ye'll ken the next time.

Noo, ony questions? Communion? Dinna you worry aboot the Communion. As Session Clerk, I mak aa the arrangements for that. Now the wine I get fae Bertie Willox, the grocer. Now I widna say it wis weak, the wine I get fae Bertie, but ye ken the parable of oor Lord turnin the water into wine? D'ye nae ken that een? Oh that's a good een, aat. Aye, it's in the Bible. Now have ye got a Bible o yer ain? Never mind, there's aye plenty lyin aboot the kirk. Have ye got a dog collar? No? In the name o . . . Weel ye'll get een at E&M's in Aiberdeen. E&M's. Next door tae Millet's, far ye got yer anorak an yer jimmies. Faar wis I? Bertie Willox the grocer and our Lord turning the water into wine. Weel, Bertie, withoot benefit of divine intervention, regularly turns the wine into water.

Noo as far as the other part of the sacrament, the loaf. That is supplied by Jimmy Kennedy the baker. Weel, he usually gies us loaf. But it jist depends on fit's left ower fan the shop shuts on Setterday. Last Communion I got a dough ring, and the wife got a bit o chocolate sponge. Weel she disna like chocolate sponge, so she swopped wi Mrs Fraser fae the Post Office – she'd got a meringue. Mind you, the Communion afore that wis even worse. The baker wis on holiday, we went to the ice-cream shop and they gave us wafers!

A Heart-Beat Away

Political fact: In the United States, Vice-president Dan Quayle is one heart-beat away from the White House. Medical fact: Heart failure can be caused by excessive laughter.

Don't make the President laugh, folks
Dan Quayle's waiting there in the wings.
Be very hesitant telling the President
Even quite humorous things.
Bob Hope's familiar 'Hey, this one'll kill yah'
Is really too risky by half;
To avoid the disaster
Of Quayle as our master
Don't make the President laugh.
George Bush ain't no Lincoln
But Quayle don't bear thinkin –
Don't make the President laugh.

The President watching strong comedy
Is something we've got to avert.
A good Barney Miller's a probable killer
And *Cheers* is an absolute cert.
Let the President hunt tiger,
Or climb up the Eiger,
Or play five sets with Steffi Graf.
Feed 'im cream, feed 'im gateau,
But not Walter Matthau –
Don't make the President laugh.
Don't let him experience
Ronald Reagan acting serious –
Don't make the President laugh.

The President must be protected
From cocktail-bar jokers and wits.
He mustn't have that pal in
Who can do Woody Allen,

49

And frequently has him in fits.
Your Bill Cosbys and Eddie Murphys
Seem safe on the surface,
But plug in that cardiograph.
One titter, one chortle
And it could be mortal –
Don't make the President laugh.
Just the hint of a grin there
And Quayle could be in there
Don't make the President laugh.

Mrs Bush, take good care of your husband;
'Tain't enough to make sure he keeps slim.
Though they find it bewild'rin', don't let his grand-children
Be cute and amusing to him.
He could be in a pickle, if you gave him a tickle –
That would be the ultimate gaffe.
In the bedroom together
Use a whip not a feather –
Don't make the President laugh.
For it's Scotland that carries
The base for Polaris;
We could all have the same epitaph.
For our chances are nuttin'
With Quayle on the button;
Don't make the President –
The new White House Resident –
Don't make the President Laugh.

Dan Quayle: US Vice-President 1988-92, best known for his inability to spell. He had particular difficulty with 'potato', to which he regularly attributed a final 'e'. Fit a tattiee! cf. Edzelle Bluee and Kerr's Pinke (p. 35).

The Eiger: Switzerland's answer to Bennachie.

Cheers: American comedy institution, played out in a bar.

Barney Miller: American comedy institution, played out in a police station.

Bob Hope: American comedy institution, played out this past whilie, we fear.

Woody Allen: Comedic, myopic, noorotic Noo Yorkite.

Ronald Reagan: President of the United States 1980-1988. Great record in show business, less happy as President.

Abraham Lincoln: President of the United States 1860-1865. Great record as President, less happy in the theatre.

The Hundred Fiddlers

A back-cloth illustrating a large Scottish fiddle orchestra. It emerges that three of the members of the orchestra are George, Buff and Steve. They sing the following words to a succession of well-known fiddle tunes.

Bonnie Lass o Bon Accord

All. It's fun
A hun-
Dred fiddlers fiddlin,
Absolutely synchronised as one –

S. One;

All. It's marv'lous how a hundred fiddlers
Play away in perfect unison –

S. Unison.

B. Oh, neen o us is formally trained,
But from childhood we have played awaa;
G. I learned it at my mither's knee.
S. I picked it up at some low joint an aa.

White Cockade

All. Seated high on planks
In our serried ranks
We come from offices and shops and banks;
Oh, a fiddler's image may be dull and staid –
G. But the bottle in my sporran isna lemonade.
All. There's a hundred o's,
An we sit gey close
An up an up an up the thermometer goes –
Ninety-nine degrees – and that is Centigrade;
G. Still the bottle in my sporran isna lemonade.

B & S. There's a Mrs Kerr
An I mean nae slur,
But ye hinna muckle room if ye're next tae her;
G. Which was why last Friday I wis affa gled
That the bottle in my sporran wisna lemonade.

51

G.   I could see
That she'd
Sat next tae me
All went well
Til her el –
Bow went in my ee

All.   But we could administer wir ain first aid –
'Cos the bottles in wir sporrans wisna lemonade.

Jig: Miss Sally Hunter of Thurston

B & S. Oh, bein a fiddler taks some skill,
'Cos fiddlin's mair tricky than playin the violin,
B.   And I include
Yehud –
I Menuhin –
He wis kicked oot o the Fiddlers.

S.   Yehudi's OK
At play –
In Brahms
B.   And yet at Scott Skinner
He's jist a beginner:
He jist canna dig
S.   A Jig,
B.   An marches are
Far ower hard for Yehudi.

All.   Though ev'ry concerto
That you've ever heard o
B.   Yehudi can play, be it Mozart or Mendelssohn;
S.   But ae day the feel
Had a go at a reel,
All.   An it jist aboot ruptured Yehudi.

Flowers of Edinburgh

All.   Ye can hae ower much o a thing nae metter fit it is,
Nae metter fit a hit it is,
However good we are;
G.   When we put on a show, therefore, we have got a policy:
To vary things we allus hae
A great big star.

B. From the south we'll bring a
Really well-known singer.
Some have said if we gave them alcohol they would.
We've had cheery Bill McCue,
And Peter Morr'son too,
Mary Sandeman and Frankie Goes To Hollywood.

G. We've had Ken McKellar
(Didna know the feller)
But he said that a tenor wis what he wid be.
Well, that made us all rejoice,
Till it clicked he meant his voice –
We had thought he meant a tenner's what his fee wid be.

S. And we've hid Mick Jagger –
He's an affa bugger.
Is there onybody wrigglier or squirmier?
In the middle o a reel
We thocht we heard a squeel –
Peer Mick hid went an gien himsel a hernia.

Flower of the Quern

Last week we appeared on Channel Four,
The channel for minority art.
Our viewing figure was ninety-four –
Six fewer than were taking part.

We're playing now a slow, sweet air
Of the kind music experts commend;
But we start off slow, and we slow doon mair.
Ye wonder if we'll mak it . . . tae . . . the . . . end.

Bonnie Banchory

Oh, the only rule o fiddlin is ye've got tae wear the kilt,
An it disna metter if it disna fit – hooch aye.
There's a kilt here on the stage that wis torpedoed at Dunkirk,
Aye, the lady playin the base is wearin it – hooch aye.

So the picture we present is very tartanny,
Though the kilt does not suit everyone's anatomy.
The conductor's got the bum for't,
Which for us is quite a comfort,
'Cos his kilt is keeping time although his baton's nae. Hooch!

Bonny Lass of Bon Accord (Reprise)

> Ta ta
> Fae aa
> The hundred fiddlers –
> Fit a lovely sound an fit a sicht;
> And now we've got wir elbows workin,
> We'll be sittin fiddlin here aa nicht.

Yehudi Menuhin: Real name Ewen Mennie fae Ythanwells, he was a big disappointment to his father, who had hoped he would be accepted for the Banchory Strathspey and Reel Society, but Willie Smith, the heid bummer of the Society wouldn't let him in because of a drink problem – he didn't stand his hand in the Burnett Arms after the audition.

Brahms, Mozart and Mendelsohn: Other foreigners also given the bum's rush by Willie Smith.

Frankie Goes to Hollywood: Misprint for 'Frankie Goes to Holyrood' – a reference to a well-known Aberdeen solicitor hoping to get a gong, but for once, we beat him to it.

Mick Jagger: Charismatic though overly demonstrative skip of the Rolling Stones, curling champions of Buchan and Formartine. 'The bugger's an affa poser.' Charlie Allan, *Press & Journal* 18 May 1988.

Doctor and Patient

Scene: Auchterturra War Memorial Hospital. A bed faces away from the audience so that the patient in it cannot be identified. Enter a Doctor (Steve).

Doc. Wakey, wakey. Mrs Thatcher.

Waken up now, waken up ma dear. It's time to tak yer sleepin tablets.

Weel by jove that's a richt black ee ye've got there.

You've fairly been in the wars, Maggie. I hope you dinna min' me caaing ye Maggie, but fin ye're a country GP yer bedside manner is sometimes the best medicine. In fact it is sometimes the only medicine.

Weel, weel we've got yer notes here: 'Precaution for concussion,' and we'll jist get the hale story fae ye.

No, no, ma dear. Dinna bother puttin in yer teeth for me, and dinna bother takkin oot yer curlers either, aat's good curlers aat. No, no, we'll jist get this reid tape oot o the wye. Now we ken yer merried name, Thatcher, but we're gaan to need yer maiden name, now. Maiden name?

Eh? Roberts! Roberts, oh there's a pucklie Roberts in Aiberdeenshire. Are ye ony connection wi the Roberts o Rothienorman?

No. Kemnay?

No, I'll tell ye there wis a family o tinker Roberts bade roon aboot Tarland for a whilie. Did yer aal man ging roon the doors selling claes-pegs?

No? Oh he wis a grocer wis he. Oh, weel, never min' fit yer aal man's occupation wis, it's your occupation that we're gaan tae need next. Fit will we put in here for your occupation now? Eh?

Housewife and dictator. Mmm.

Now next question. Next-of-kin? Faa div we get in touch wi if ye kick the bucket? Nae that there's ony fear o that. Mercy me, the standards in this hospital. We've never lost a patient yet. Weel nae since the case o Charlie Geddes, an Charlie didna conk oot. He jist ran aff wi the nicht sister. Aye, I think she wis in a huff aboot her gradin. No, no, this next-of-kin is jist a formality.

Eh? Mr Thatcher. Of course, of course, Mr Dennis Thatcher. Aha. An fit wye div we get a hud o Dennis noo? Is he up in these parts wi ye? Oh he is. Good, and hiv ye got a telephone number for him? Oh ye hiv. Ballater Golf Club. Mmm-hmmm . . . Extension 19. Mmm . . .

Noo next question – purpose of visit? Aye, fit brings ye to Auchterturra Maggie?

Eh? Oh ye wis up for the wikend at Balmoral. God, ye didna get that black ee at Balmoral did ye?

Oh ye wis at the Games at Braemar. Aha.

An accident wi a heavy hammer.

Eh? Oh, nae a heavy hammer. A heavy handbag, and ye're nae sure if it wis an accident. Ye think the Queen meant tae hit ye. Never mind, ye're here, ye're here. They brocht ye straight to Auchterturra War Memorial Hospital.

No, no ma dear, that wisna an ambulance that brocht ye. It was a tractor. Dod Walker's tractor. And ye're jist lucky that it's next wik that he starts the dung spreadin.

His eye is caught by a dish of grapes from which a card protrudes.

God, aat's affa fine lookin grapes.

He takes one and eats it.

Ugh! It's affa soor. Faa gave ye that soor grapes?

(*Reads card*) 'Best wishes, Ted Heath.'

Oh well noo, that's the kind o grapes that ye should be sharin roon. Faa's the lady in the next bed?

Oh it's nae a lady, it's Willie Duff, the butcher.

Eh, fit's aat. Fit's Willie in for?

Weel Willie's in 'cos he got his thumb stuck in the mincer, so fin the denner comes roon my advice is keep aff the shepherd's pie.

Oh aye, here we go. Aye, patients' queries. Yes. Is there anything you would like to ask me? Is there onything ye're nae sure aboot?

There is absolutely nothing in this world that you are not sure about.

Oh, well, is there onything else ails ye quine?

Eh? You think that ye've got a grumbling appendix. God, I'm surprised it's got the nerve.

Mrs Thatcher: Invited to appear in this sketch as herself. Mrs Thatcher gave us the thumbs down, or rather, having just entered her Churchillian phase, the fingers up.

The Bottle Bank

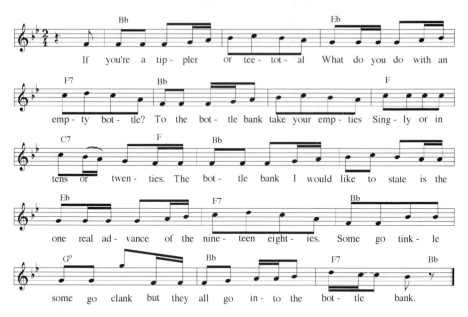

If you're a tippler or teetotal,
What do you do with an empty bottle?
To the bottle-bank take your empties
Singly or in tens or twenties;
The bottle-bank I would like to state is
The one real advance of the 1980s
Some go tinkle, some go clank,
But they all go into the bottle-bank.

A man comes along very late at night
With a hundred empties –
Well, not quite,
And his clerical collar concealed from sight,
And his sins disappear in the bottle-bank.
A Salvation Army girl is seen,
Chucking in empties, quite serene,
All to the sound of a tambourine,
As she pops them into the bottle-bank.
A chap who's clearly had a party
Brought his bottles in a horse and cartie,
I thought as I patted that horse's flank:
This must be the Clyesdale bottle-bank.

Here comes a guy with a dozen or more –
Poor chap he doesn't know the score.
He hasn't put 'em in,
Oh no, he's stackin' 'em,
Thinking he'll get tuppence back on 'em.

Here comes one of Britain's head men,
Nigel Lawson with a crate full of dead men;
All soft drinks, but how ironic:
Most of them are slim line tonic.

TIA MARIA –
A bottle of Tia Maria,
Put in by Auntie Jean,
Who swears she's always been
TT.
Here's Ken Dodd with bottles various –
How extremely tattifilarious.
I asked him, 'Isn't your bottle bank in
Jersey or the Isle of Man, Ken?'

Down to the depths with the self-same thonk
Descend the vintage and the plonk;
Champagne bottles from classy cellars
Perish beside Valpolicellas.

Next with a load comes Tam Dalyell –
You can see that he's partial to Moselle.
He sinks Moselle, he sinks Cinzano;
But did he sink the General Belgrano?

Ponder this: No man or woman
Should despise a fellow human.
Beer is humble, Burgundy's swank –
But they end up together in the bottle-bank.

Slim line tonic: It clearly worked. From being a terrible fattie in 1988, Nigel could now pass for a reincarnation of Lord Home of the Hirsel.

King James

It is 1603, the year of the Union of the Crowns and the new King James VI and I (Buff) is having a hard day at the office.

King James: (*telephoning*) Hello, Stratford on Avon 2322? Can I speak to Mr William Shakespeare, please? Oh, it's yourself. Hello, Bill. Jimmy here. Jimmy Stewart. No, not that Jimmy Stewart. Nothing to do with the Glenn Miller Story. This is the King. I'm speaking from London. Aye. I used to be in Edinburgh, but I got a wee promotion down here to Head Office.

So how goes it, Bill? Long time no see. I think the last time I saw you was when you were up in Scotland touring with *Allo, allo*. I bumped into you on the Waverley Steps. Aye, they're still as draughty. What? It was on the Waverley Steps that you got the idea for the Tempest. I'm not surprised. So have you been back to Edinburgh since then? You were up in a Variety Show? With Cliff Richard? You must be older than you look. And while you were up you did some research for a telly thing you were doing. Say that again, Bill. You wrote the first ten episodes of *Take the High Road*. Then you put them all together and called it *Much Ado About Nothing*.

So how are you all, Bill? How's Anne and the children? Good, aye, we're all fine. We're having a bit of a problem with the son and heir – he always wants everything done his way. I have to keep telling him, 'Look, you'll be king yourself some day – Charles I. When you are, don't be too pushy, or you'll get your head in your hands to play with.'

Bill, you'll be wondering why I'm phoning. Well, have you seen your *Times* this morning? Situations Vacant? Have you not? Well, listen to this: 'Applications are invited for the post of Director of the Edinburgh International Festival. The successful candidate will have a wide knowledge of the arts' – Yes, that's right, Bill, a complete change of policy. 'Pension scheme, luncheon vouchers, company sedan chair, bla bla bla', but never mind the advert, the point is, Bill, the job's yours if you want it. Well, I admire your attitude, Bill, but there's no need to have scruples. That's the way we fill all the top jobs. Oh, we'll go through all the hoops – shortlisting, interviews and all that nonsense. But that's just to show there's nothing underhand about it.

So what about it, Bill? Well, who could do it better? Who? But he's Scottish. Are you suggesting a Scot for a top Arts job in Scotland? Bill, you're off your scone. I mean, it's a very novel idea, but it's just not on. No, it's not a written rule. It's a lot stronger than that.

Anyway, as I said to Ian Lang last week coming down on the shuttle, 'Ian,' I said, 'I know you're only the Scottish Secretary so you don't have much say in what goes on in Scotland, but when you cast your vote on the Appointments Committee for the Edinburgh Festival job, it's got to be William Shakespeare.' Well, he put down his *Daily Record* and he said, 'You'd better tell Norman here. He's got more clout than I have. And gosh, who was sitting next to him but Norman Lamont, or as they call him up in Shetland, 'peerie Norrie Lamont'. The Chancellor, aye. No, he wasn't reading the *Daily Record*. He was reading the *Sunday Post*. I said to him, 'I thought you'd be reading the *Financial Times*'. He said, 'No, I can never understand a word of the *Financial Times*. I mean, do you know what the Dow Jones Index is. Does anybody know what the Dow Jones Index is?' Anyway, when I said to him, 'Will you vote for William Shakespeare?' he said, 'William who?' And I said, 'Shakespeare. Have you never heard of Shakespeare? And you went to Loretto?' He said, 'Yes, I was at Loretto. But I don't remember a Shakespeare there. Did he play rugby?'

But getting back to yourself, Bill, what are you up to at the moment? Writing a new play. *The Merchant of Venice*. No, I couldn't wangle you an Arts Council Grant for that. No, your stuff's of far too high a standard to attract Arts Council funding. For an Arts Council grant, you've got to be experimental or innovative or just plain rotten. But have you thought of private sponsorship? I mean, if the Royal Bank can sponsor the Rugby, I don't see why the Clydesdale can't sponsor *The Merchant of Venice*. God knows, they've had their pound of flesh often enough.

Anyway, Bill, you've got all the qualifications for the Edinburgh Festival job. So what about it? I mean, bear in mind the Director of the Edinburgh Festival is paid by the District Council so you've no worries, you'll get your salary on the dot every month. What? Any chance of what? Profit-sharing? Profit? Bill, it's the Edinburgh Festival we're talking about.

William Shakespeare (1564-1616): Prolific English writer, a kind of English James Kelman without the swear words.

'Allo, allo': Translated from 'Bonjour, bonjour,' a little-known comedy by Moliére (1622-73).

Charles I: Name of first British King to be called Charles. A little later there was a Charles II. But will there ever be a Charles III?

Ian Lang: Matinee idol, very popular at Shakespeare's Globe Theatre.

The Ozone Layer

In the bustle and strife
Of contemp'rary life
As we race and chase and scurry about,
On the merry-go-round
Anxieties abound
There's so many things to worry about:
Should you eat creamy cheese?
Should you buy Japanese?
Should you be a poll-tax payer?
Would you stop, if you please,
Getting knotted up by these,
And worry about the ozone layer.
Don't be trivial or small,
If you worry at all,
Worry about the ozone layer.

The day may occur
When the bank manager
Says your overdraft's not funny,
And you're stuck in a phase
Of financial malaise –
What the hell? it's only money.
Don't feel sick or harassed
If your mortgage is vast
And your hair is getting greyer.
Though you've spent ev'ry cent,
That's a big non-event,
Worry about the ozone layer.

Don't, we insist,
Get your knickers in a twist
About the bank rate or inflation;
And don't lose your smalls
If Forsyth makes a balls
Of your children's education.
If you find out one day
That your sons both are gay
And your wife is even gayer,
Never mind things like that,
Show concern where it's at,
And worry about the ozone layer.

Don't you get psyched
Up because you're disliked
By the guy who's your employer,
And if you're dismissed
'Cos you're permanently drunk,
That's no cause for paranoia.
If, though once quite devout
You're invaded now by doubt
And you've lost your faith in prayer,
Does it matter a jot
Whether God exists or not?
Worry about the ozone layer.

Where we live, what we earn,
That's the kind of concern
That our modern life-style sends us.
Are you coping with sex?

Should you get stronger specs?
Should you switch to contact lenses?
If you're losing your looks,
If you break out in plooks,
Never mind, you shouldn't care,
Thinning hair, double chin –
Just ignore them and begin
To worry about the ozone layer.

Don't sit and brood
About the dangers of food,
Oriental, French, Hellenic.
Whatever you consume
Some prophet of doom
Will pronounce it carcinogenic.
Don't get distraught
At the food you have bought
From your frozen food purveyor.
It's only listeria,
Curb your hysteria,
And worry about the ozone layer.
If there's one thing should scare us all,
Go easy on the aerosol
And worry about the ozone layer.
Yours may seem a serene house,
But we're all in the green house.
Let's all worry about the ozone layer.
Worry about the ozone –
Make sure this planet goes on –
Worry about the ozone layer.

Closing Reprise
With the lights up a notch –
There, you've glanced at your watch,
Don't imagine you disguised it.
You've remembered how far
You've to walk to your car,
Maybe someone's vandalised it.
And there's much worse than that
May have happened at your flat
While you've been sitting there.
Don't get anxious over these
Petty possibilities – Worry about the ozone layer.

The Indian Restaurateur

A radio D.J. (Buff) is interviewing a studio guest (Steve).

D.J. We all like to pop along to our local Indian restaurant now and again for a curry. Indian restaurants are part of our way of life. With me tonight is someone who has reversed the trend – a young Aberdonian home on holiday from India, where two years ago he opened the first Scottish restaurant in Calcutta. Hello.

S.G. Hello, good evening and very warm greetings from Calcutta.

D.J. Now you're home visiting your parents?

S.G. Yes, my father Sarendra Gandhi still runs the Taj Mahal Restaurant in Justice Mill Lane, just aside the Uptown Baths yonder. That was where I started my career in the catering racket – trade.

D.J. And of course your father married a local girl.

S.G. Yes, he did marry her. A very honourable man, my father. My mother is from Auchterturra. She is an Auchterturra quine. She was a Thomson.

D.J. Oh, she was a Thomson. Was she . . . ?

S.G. Yes, she was a daughter of the great Sandy.

D.J. Oldmeldrum Sports, Ballater Toy Shop?

S.G. That's right. He's a helluva man, old Sandy. I am called after him.

D.J. So your name is?

S.G. Sandy Gandhi. And when I was a loon I spent half my time in the restaurant and half my time oot on the ferm – pliterin aboot in the sharn.

D.J. I would have thought that was unpleasant for you.

S.G. You never saw the kitchen in the restaurant. No, that is a joke. It is a very fine restaurant.

D.J. But you didn't think of opening your own Indian Restaurant in Scotland?

S.G. Oh, no! In Scotland you canna get moved for Indian restaurants. So I say to myself, 'Sandy,' I say, 'Get yokit. Play the Scottish card in India.'

D.J. Why India?

S.G. Aha! I use the heid. I think to myself – all these Indian restaurants in Scotland: nae cooks left in India. I will fill the gap in the market. I will do what Maggie Thatcher says – be an entrepreneur.

D.J. And you sell Scottish food in Calcutta?

S.G. That is correct. I cannot stand Indian food. The curries are far too hot. I dinna ken fit wye folk can eat them that hot.

D.J. So what do you serve?

S.G. We do a special high tea for four persons. Or you can order four dishes separately: fish and chips, haggis and neeps, toad in the hole and stovies. Put them all in the middle of the table an aabody has a suppie.

D.J. But if I wanted a three-course meal?

S.G. Well, you could have Scotch Broth, Scotch Egg, Scotch Trifle, and, from the wine list, Scotch. For a starter, you have heard of the traditional Scottish delicacy – second day's soup. We go one better – we offer third day's soup.

D.J. Third day's?

S.G. Well, it takes two days to fly it out from Crosse & Blackwell's.

D.J. And for a main course?

S.G. Our principal main course is stovies. Just like on an Indian menu where you get thirty or forty different kinds of curry, so on my menu there are thirty or forty different kinds of stovies. Look – Numbers 23 to 59, all stovies.

D.J. I know what you mean by the different kinds of curries. My favourite is Madras Curry Ghosh.

S.G. That's right. My stovies are the same – Stovies Ghosh, Stovies Goodness Gracious, Stovies Crikey, Stovies Losh be Here, right up to Stovies Godalmichty.

D.J. I see, and do you pursue the parallel with curry? I mean, with the stovies are there accompaniments?

S.G. Oh yes. We've got a record of Jimmy Shand and his band playing.

D.J. And since your customers are mainly Indian, do you serve the stovies vindaloo?

S.G. Wherever the customer wants them. But I would not recommend the loo. The kitchen is bad enough. However, whatever the customer wants – after all, he who pays the piper calls the tune.

D.J. You haven't a piper?

S.G. Oh yes, we keep an old Gordon Highlander in the bothy. Get him in a good mood efter twaa or three drams and he'll play the spoons as well.

D.J. I like the look of No. 93 – chapati.

S.G. No, no. Not chapati. Chappit tatties.

D.J. Do you serve *them* in a sauce?

S.G. Not exactly in a sauce. But there are bottles on the table. Tomato, Worcester, Mayonnaise.

D.J. HP?

S.G. Oh no. Cash only. Some of these Indians are real cowboys.

D.J. Well, here's something that's served in a sauce. No. 83, Forfar Bridie in tomato sauce. Good grief! It's the most expensive thing on the menu.

S.G. Well, it's the extra labour costs.

D.J. How d'you mean?

S.G. It's a helluva job getting the bridie into the bottle.

Radio D.J.: When this sketch was brought to life on television, it was daringly and spectacularly opened out to take place in the only Buchan bistro in Bombay. It then became the pilot for *Jewel in the Crown*, but when that prestigious series came to be made, Buff and Steve – simply because they were perceived as being more Dufton Scott than Paul Scott – were shamefully overlooked.

Life's not Easy

Life's not easy – the world can be very spiteful,
The business of living is frightful,
Life's not easy.
Life's not easy – the human condition is dire,
OK I'm a Jeremiah,
Life's not easy.
Life's a trial,
Frequently I just can't crack it.
I know I'll
Struggle to open a biscuit packet.
Life is full of snags and snares:
How do you find the start of the sellotape?
I never can.

Life's not easy – I mean it, I wouldn't kid yah,
Can you preset a video?
Life's not easy.
Life's not easy – there's nothing that makes me tenser
Than using a soap dispenser,
Life's not easy.
Mayonnaise
Won't come out so you thump the bottle,
Life's rule says:
None'll come out or else the lot'll.
Things like that can bring a frown –
I drop a scone and always it lands with its
Jammy side down.

When a bottle of pills, as it ought to have,
Has a fiendish childproof top on it,
I'm completely stumped, and I've got to have
The help of a child to open it.

Life's not easy – there's dozens of situations
Designed to test your patience – life's not easy.
Life's not easy – a toffee, but can you scoff it?
You can't get the paper off it – life's not easy.
On the phone
Nothing makes me quite so nervous
As the tone
That tells you to speak to an answering service;
All my thoughts just seem to go.
New toaster blows – but where is the guarantee?
I never know.

Life's not easy: my train leaves at 20 hundred.
That's 10 o'clock – no, I've blundered! Life's not easy.
Life's not easy, it sure can be a glum thing,
To get through the day is something – life's not easy
Ev'ry Christmas
Where have the lights for the tree been lurking?
Same old business –
One of them's loose, so none of them's working.
Life's a bowl of raspberries –
Choosing a choc'late, can you dodge the marzipan?
I never can.
Life's not easy.

The Fish Farmer

Interviewer (Buff): I'm joined now by Mr Torquil McKenzie (Steve), recently voted Highland Businessman of the Year. To have won that award, you must be one of the most formidable, dynamic, charismatic figures ever to burst upon the Highlands?

McK.   Aye, right enough.

Int.   What exactly is it you do?

McK.   A bit of this and a bit of that. I'm always willin to take a risk. A couple of years ago I asked myself, 'What's the biggest risk I can take?' And that was the start of McKenzie (Nuclear Waste Dumping) Ltd.

Int.   Nuclear waste? And where did you dump it?

McK.   At the bottom of the garden. But it was a big mistake. The dog kept scrapin it up.

Int.   But it turned out okay?

McK.   Aye. Soon after that I cornered the market in two-headed dogs. And after that I never looked back. It's more than you can say for the dog.

Int.   So that set you up as it were. And what's your latest enterprise?

McK.   Well it's a fish farm on Loch Ness.

Int.   A fish farm? And how does fish farming differ from ordinary farming?

McK.   Ach, not a lot. Mind you, with all that water, yer tractor gets helluva rusty.

Int.   And is it salmon mostly that you . . .

McK.   No, it's not salmon. It's tadpoles.

Int.   Tadpoles?

McK.   Tadpoles.

Int.   And what's the technology of farming tadpoles?

McK. You need a helluva lot of jam-jars. So thank the Lord me and the wife eat a helluva lot o jam. Raspberry mainly.

Int. I didn't know people ate tadpoles.

McK. Oh, aye. The wife does a very tasty tadpole omelette. Then she does a special gourmet tadpole taramasalata.

Int. Tell me, does she smoke them?

McK. Well, she's experimentin, you know. But they keep wrigglin out of her clay pipe. Unless she's really quick lightin up.

Int. I must say it's hard to believe there's any commercial potential in tadpoles.

McK. There's a lot of folk take tadpoles with a pinch of salt. But there's a future in tadpoles. Your humble tadpole's going to grow into something big. Like a frog: just the other day I was about to stick my fork into one and it changed into a puddock and louped off my plate. Now, you don't get that kind of thing with a pork chop.

Int. You mentioned this fish farm of yours is on Loch Ness?

McK. Loch Ness, aye.

Int. Have you had any adventures there?

McK. Well just the other week there I pulled out this great huge thing 40ft. long, with an enormous head and five massive humps on its back.

Int. What did you do?

McK. I threw it back. You could never get a thing like that in a jam-jar.

Aye, right enough: Multi-purpose Inverness expression used sometimes to signify agreement, but more often to demonstrate that the idle Highlander who is speaking – ever happy, sensible fellow, to follow the line of least resistance – is at least still awake. (When we asked an Inverness friend if he thought this sentence was a tad complex and not readily comprehensible, he replied, 'Aye, right enough.')

Tadpole taramasalata: Drumnadrochit delicacy enthusiastically praised by Derek Cooper in 'Scotland's Larder', 1996.

The Prince of Wales
(Tune: We'll keep a welcome on the hillsides)

We'll always welcome new developments
As lang as commonsense prevails,
As lang's they dinna dae awaa wi
Treasures like the Prince of Wales.
O, the planners have a vision
And they will tell you fancy tales,
But surely nothing justifies
Daein awaa wi the Prince of Wales;

Oh they shouldna, wouldna, couldna
Dae awaa
Wi the Prince of Wales.

Prince of Wales: Venerable Aberdeen pub. This passionate prayer to preserve it had the deserved effect, and the pub continues to flourish. Scotland the What? are still waiting for the proprietor to express his gratitude in some tangible way.

City of Culture

books an' gaun tae plays My life's one lang frus - tra - tion. 'Cos

rall............

now - a - days she tak's no heed o' The cry - ing needs of my li - bi - do She in -

sists on dis - cuss - in' Oth - ell - o She tells me Pic - ass - o's a

must Well what good is that tae a fel - la Con -

sumed by a good go - in' lust. There's no much that's a - rous - in' in a

chat a - boot Stock - hau - sen or a play by Ar - nold Wes - ker. Oh I'm

Ever since that marvellous day when we
Were told that Glesca wis gaan tae be
The European city of culture,
I somehow dinna click the same
Wi Fran, my wee Drumchapel flame
My advances seem tae insult 'er;

'Cos suddenly I find
It's matters of the mind
That are her preoccupation,
She's cultured nowadays,
Readin books and gaan tae plays,
My life's one lang frustration;
'Cos nowadays she taks nae heed o
The cryin needs o my libido.

She insists on discussin Othella,
She tells me Picasso's a must.
Well, what good is that tae a fella
Consumed by a good-goin lust?
There's nae much that's arousin
In a chat aboot Stockhausen
Or a play by Arnold Wesker,
Oh, I'm lumbered wi a lassie
Wha's baith cultural and classy,
And they're aa like that in Glesca.

1990 is not far away now,
And culture's abroad in the air,
And carnal pursuits are passé now,
I'm one that's nae gettin his share.
My bird talks aa day leng
In an Edinburgh tweng
Of the art of Medagescar;
She wis sexy once and tarty,
Now she's cerebral and arty,
An they're aa like that in Glesca.

Now I dinna easy embarrass,
Dismissin maist things wi a smile,
But recently doon at the barras
She asked me my views on Kurt Weil.
She's a raver – people snigger
At her well-upholstered figure,
She could not be statuesquer.
But her passion is for Ibsen
And Sir Alexander Gibson,
And they're aa like that in Glesca.

Now I'm nae the kind that wid stir it,
But nowadays when I get fresh,
She's on aboot things o the spirit
An there's never nae sins o the flesh.
Aa the birds in Carntyne are
Whistlin fugues in C sharp minor –
Things could not be much grotesquer.
Yer ardour dis get caaler
When she says, 'Let's play some Mahler'
An they're aa like that in Glesca.

I read all the scandalous bits in
The Mirror, the Star and *the Sun,*
But she really likes Solzenhitsyn –
She's readin the *Gulag* for fun.
Her name is Fran McLure –
Aye, for years that's how I knew 'er,
Now she cries hersel Francesca.
I wid like tae tak my girrel
Tae the boozer no the Burrell,
But they're aa like that –
Every bird's a culture cat
They're aa like that in Glesca.

Solzenhitsyn: Rangers' Siberian right winger. Frequently yellow-carded for dissent.

City of Culture: The whole song is a lament suitable for rendition by Glasgow's greatest cultural ikon, pictured below, by the way.

Mastermind
(Mastermind Theme Music)

Magnus Magnusson (Buff): Good evening and welcome once again to *Mastermind* which comes this week from Aberdeen's leading educational establishment, Quarryhill Primary School. As ever on *Mastermind* there are four contenders. Could we have the first contender please. (*enter Sandy Thomson: Steve*) Your name?

S.T.   Sandy Thomson

M.M.   Occupation?

S.T.   Retired futret tamer.

M.M.   And your specialist subject?

S.T.   'Petty crime in Auchterturra – May tae June 1988.'

M.M.   A very wide subject indeed, Mr Thomson – you have two minutes on 'Petty Crime in Auchterturra' between those dates starting NOW.

On May 10th, in the Spar grocer, Tam the poacher pinched something – what was it that he pinched?

S.T.   Bella Bruce's bottom.

M.M.   Correct.

On may 16th, what crime was committed by the Dominie's twelve-year-old twin sons?

S.T.   Gaan twaa on a bike.

M.M.   Correct.

Why didn't PC Wilson pursue the boys?

S.T.   It was his bike.

M.M.   Correct.

On May 22nd, Willie McGill was charged with forging the bank manager's

name but he was acquitted; what was his special defence?

S.T. He couldna write his ain name.

M.M. That's not quite enough.

S.T. The bunker couldna write at aa.

M.M. Correct.

On May 29th, Eddie Jack, the Auchterturra plumber, was on holiday near Killicrankie, when he was stopped for speeding. Where exactly did the offence take place?

S.T. Pass.

M.M. Correct.

On June 1st, who in Auchterturra was driving without a licence or insurance?

S.T. Aabody wis.

M.M. Correct.

There are two cells at the police station. Both of them were occupied for the whole of June. By whom?

S.T. The bobby's wife's summer visitors.

M.M. Correct.

In the case of the procurator fiscal versus Hamish Anderson, Anderson was charged with breaking into Bella Bruce's bedroom at 2am. What was the verdict?

S.T. Guilty, but insane.

M.M. Correct.

In June, what crime in Auchterturra remained undetected?

S.T. Illegal removal from clothes-lines aa ower the village o sundry items of ladies underwear.

M.M. That's not what I have here.

S.T. Knickers bein nicked?

M.M. Correct.

And although the police never caught the knicker thief, were there any suspects?

S.T. Oh, thir wir nae suspects. Aabody in the village kent it wis the postie.

M.M. Correct.

At the Auchterturra Sports Jock Findlay won two events, drinking eight pints in thirty seconds followed by the eighty yards dash. He then committed a public nuisance. What exactly did he do?

S.T. Pass.

M.M. Correct.

Also at the Auchterturra Sports, Walter Rattray did a streak through the WRI tent. What was the result?

S.T. He won first prize in the dried fruit.

M.M. Correct.

On June 13th, three people were drunk and disorderly outside the Glaikit Stirk public house. Two of them were Eddie Jack the plumber and Willie Duff the butcher. Who was the third?

S.T. It wis me!

M.M. Correct.

On June 16th, Dougal MacKenzie and Jean Geddes crept into Tam MacFarlane's hayloft where they were discovered by PC Wilson. When the constable told Dougal to stop what he was doing, how did Dougal reply? BEEP. BEEP. BEEP. BEEP. (*Buzzer*)

S.T. I've started an I canna stop.

Quarryhill Primary School: The identity of the educational institution varied according to where we were doing the sketch. In Glasgow, in September 1995, it was Bearsden Academy, where a certain sixth-form pupil turned out to be a thirty-two-year-old, prompting Magnus to say, 'This afternoon we met some of the Academy's senior pupils some of whom were nearly senior citizens.'

Neighbours

Buff.   Neighbours –
We've got bloody awful neighbours.
I've complained tae them politely,
But it's never ony use.
She is
Even nestier than he is –
That pair o charmers that bide through the hoose.

Steve. Neighbours –
We're tormented by oor neighbours,
She is Tory, he is Labour,
And they've baith a hell'va thirst.
Twaa cans o beer in,
An he's thumpin her and sweirin.
Three gins an ginger,
'N she'll injure
Him first.

Buff.   Their name is Harker,
She's an affa Nosey Parker
Wi a look o Ronnie Barker,
And her nose could use a dicht.
He's just a gype, and
He's a drummer in a pipe band,
And what is worse is
He rehearses
Aa nicht.

Steve. Fan they came hee-er,
They'd a poodle caad Maria,
Very prone to diarrhoea –
Nae a dog ye could ignore.
But they had trained it
So it didna foul the pavement,
Instead it whoopsied
Jist ootside
Oor door.

Buff. Cleo –
That's her name and his is Leo,
And they've baith got affa B.O.
Even grimmer than their looks.
She's like a Sumo,
Punches harder than Frank Bruno,
He's mair like Hitler
But littler
Wi plooks.

George. Neighbours –
I've got baith o them for neighbours,
They are baith commercial traivellers,
Him for sweeties, him for gin.
Their wives are randy,
Very keen on hooch-ma-gandie.
Fan they're awaa
I have twaa
Bidies in.

All. Picture your neighbours
Through the hoose or up the stai-ers –
Ye're bloomin lucky if they're your
Friends.

Neighbours: The tune is not a million miles from the signature tune of a well-known Australian soap opera of that name. You're apt to see the closing seconds of it, if you make the mistake of switching on a little early for the Six o'clock News.

Frank Bruno: Heavyweight boxing champion, briefly of the world, annually of the Empire (Croydon) – Babes in the Wood 1993, Aladdin 1994, Jack and the Beanstalk 1995, Cinderella 1996, available 1997.

Ronnie Barker: Heavyweight TV comedy champion – star of *Open All Hours* and *Porridge*, and – in body-weight – four-fifths of *The Two Ronnies*.

Election '99

Haig Gordon (Buff) speaks to camera.

H.G. Good evening, and welcome to Election Special, 1999. 1999 – already a momentous year because of the resignation of Mrs Margaret Thatcher after a mere twenty years in power. Yes, it will be recalled that there was a crisis of leadership in 1990, but that was a mere blip in the print-out of history. Mrs Thatcher overcame it by declaring war for a second time on Argentina, following the non-appearance of Diego Maradona in the match against Scotland at Hampden. As Mrs Thatcher said, 'That's the kind of insult we in Scotland won't tolerate.' But now in 1999 she has resigned, and last week on this programme we watched her waving farewell from the steps of the space shuttle which travels from Glasgow to Jupiter via Prestwick. She was off to meet her latest challenge – the sorting out of the rest of the Universe, because – in her own words – 'God has been getting a bit sloppy lately. And a bit Bolshie too. Who does he think he is – Ted Heath?'

And this General Election of 1999 is all about choosing Mrs Thatcher's successor. Waiting for me now are the two main candidates, both of whom, as it happens, are Scots. I'm joined first of all by the new leader of the Conservative Party, Mr Malcolm Rifkind.

Mr Rifkind, if you were to become Prime Minister, what difference would it make to you personally?

M.R. Well, of course, as might reasonably be expected, I would be even more pleased with myself than I am at the moment. And I say that in all modesty.

H.G. Could there be a problem if you become PM? There'd be no-one available to be Secretary of State.

M.R. Spotted that one. I would appoint somebody from the House of Lords. Lord Boothby.

H.G. Lord Boothby's dead.

M.R. They'd never notice that in the Lords.

H.G. Of course some of us can remember Nineteen-EIGHTY-nine, when out of a total of 72 Scottish MPs 10 were Tories.

M.R. Happy days. I do wish we still enjoyed the same measure of popular support.

H.G. Yes, because by the end of the last Parliament you were the only one left.

M.R. Yes, after Nicky Fairbairn went full-time into dress-making.

H.G. I thought he went to the House of Lords.

M.R. No. House of Fraser.

H.G. Mr Rifkind, thank you. I'd now like to turn to the new leader of the Labour Party, Mr Donald Dewar.

H.G. Mr Dewar, what qualities do you think you would bring to the job of Prime Minister?

D.D. Well, if I may say so, Kirsty, there are three in particular. Firstly, Kirstly, er – Kirsty, the ability to see things clearly.

H.G. Well, you're not seeing me very clearly. I'm not Kirsty Wark. I'm Haig Gordon.

D.D. Secondly, Kirsty, the ability to listen to what people say to me. And thirdly, Kirdly, er – Kirsty, the ability to communicate, er um simply and articulately and er um concisely and er um . . .

H.G. Fluently?

D.D. Fluently and without any hesitation or flaffing and er um humming and hawing in the manner associated with Neil Kinnock.

H.G. Neil Kinnock?

D.D. Predecessor of mine as Leader of the Labour Party.

H.G. Ah, Neil Kinnock.

D.D. Now Lord Boyo of Glenys.

H.G. Ah, yes, after he left Parliament he went back to Wales and has transformed its environment.

D.D. It's got a lot more wind now.

H.G. Now you have said you will be a Prime Minister for Scotland. What for instance would you do with the BBC?

D.D. I'll move it holus bolus up to Edinburgh.

H.G. Appoint a new Chairman?

D.D. Yes, Rikki Fulton.

H.G. Ah, good old Rikki Fulton.

D.D. As he now is. Lord Fulton of Auld Reekie, as I would make him.

H.G. As a committed Socialist, Mr Dewar, how do you see yourself getting on with King Charles?

D.D. Very well. No problem at all. Only yesterday I was with King Charles at a dinner given in his honour by the RIBA.

H.G. Was he on the toast list?

D.D. No, he was on the menu.

H.G. But this election may not be just a two-horse race. The SNP is now a real force. The charismatic Jim Sillars, once the member for Govan, sat in the last Parliament as SNP member for Cheltenham and Leamington Spa. Yesterday our cameras caught up with him campaigning in the streets of Scotland's new capital.

J.S. And so I say to you good people of Auchterturra – Ich bien Auchterturra-er. Ask not what Auchterturra can do for you. Ask what you can do for Auchterturra. And I will tell you. In this election vote for Auchterturra's Scottish Nationalist candidate, Antonio Guiseppe Signorini, Scotland's World Champion ice-creamer. Make Auchterturra's champion 99 man Westminster's 1999 man. Because make no mistake, this year the Scottish people are moving towards their destiny, towards a great sea change which is taking place in the watershed. Tonight I could have been in a warm TV studio enjoying a cup of coffee with Kirsty Wark. But I am not. I am here in this God-forsaken hole at the back of beyond. And why am I here? Do I fear Kirsty Wark? Did I fear Margaret Thatcher? I fear no female dictator, I am here (*very meekly*) 'cos Margo telt me tae come here.

via Prestwick: At this point Glasgow was not licensed as a transatlantic terminal but Prestwick was, so that the first lap of any flight from Glasgow to the United States was of a length more appropriate to Trans-Buchan Airways (q.v. p. 21)

Crisis of leadership in 1990: Many a true word . . . When 1990 came Mrs Thatcher experienced rather more than a crisis of leadership. Would we were half as good at prophesysing the result of the lottery.

Malcolm Rifkind: MR demonstrated his political affiliations by sporting a blue rosette and sitting with his right leg crossed over his left; in a blinding theatrical coup he turned magically into Donald Dewar by simultaneously converting his blue rosette into a red one (costume illusion and design: Anne and James Logan) and crossing his left leg over his right. As a result of these enthusiastic contortions, Steve had to have a hip replacement (Dec. 1991), with the tragic consequence that the sketch was never performed again.

Lord Chancellor's Song
(Tune: Iolanthe, Act II)

When I was a bairn and I lived at Clashfern
And my father looked after the station,
I never foresaw I would take up the law,
But the law did become my vocation.

In England the law has got many a flaw
It would take sev'ral hours to list 'em,
But who would have thought that it needed a Scot
To sort out the whole English system?

That pair of old ravers, Lords Hailsham and Havers,
Had made such a terrible mess of it,
Mrs Thatcher agreed to go north of the Tweed
To get someone to make a success of it.

For, when put to the test, we, the Scots, are the best;
There's no other nation can top us.
My forte is law, and I've mastered it 'aw' –
Decree nisi and *habeus corpus*.

As a lawyer, I may in all modesty say
That my stature is rather Wagnerian,
But I do have a quirk – I belong to a kirk
That is known as the Free Presbyterian.

The kirk that I've picked has got rules that are strict,
Unbending and not at all vapoury,
And the sternest of these lays down to Wee Frees
Not to have any contact with Papery.

And it cameth to pass I attended a Mass
For my colleague, the learned Lord Wheatley,
And – it may not make sense – but the Kirk took offence,
It got up their noses completely.

And the powers that be in the Kirk of Wee Free
Got stroppy and nasty and sharp – it
Don't often occur that the Lord Chancellor
Is – let's face it, folks – up on the carpet.

We came face to face and I pled my own case,
I could not have been better defended;
But my advocacy didn't benefit me
I finished up being suspended.

So I've had to bear a most dreadful nightmare
Considerably more hideous, I fancy,
Than the image of hell which, remember, befell
My counterpart in *Iolanthe*.

I'm no special case; it's a general disgrace –
In fact, to be blunt it's baloney –
That anyone should be divinely pursued
For paying his respects to a crony.

But I am no saint and I have no complaint,
Well, apart to be honest from this one:
Could God ever be really angry with me
For behaving just like a good Christian?

Lord Chancellor: In medieval times there were Lord Chancellors who died at the stake and on the block, but this one, Lord Mackay of Clashfern, is the only one in recorded history to suffer the extremely painful fate of being suspended by the Wee Frees.

Lords Hailsham and Havers: Two previous incumbents of the office of Lord Chancellor. Hailsham was in office much the longer and so, by definition, did a lot more havering than Havers.

Headlines 1988

(Tune: Reputations. Vol. 1 p. 270)

All. To-night is Hogmanay –
Let's look back and relate
The stories that made the headlines
In 1988.

Fergie had a baby –
A princess, nae a prince;
The bairn wis born in August
And she's hardly seen it since.

G. The Liberal and Democrat merger –
Their new name caused a tizz;
S. Even Paddy Ashdown
Can't remember what it is.
B. For Scotland's Labour members
Govan was a sign
G. No more the Feeble Fifty –
S. (They're) the Feeble 49.

B. Ben Johnson and Ed Moses
In the Seoul Olympics ran
S. Ben Johnson said, 'Hey, Moses,
Have you got the tablets, man?'
B. Lester Piggot got oot o prison
Twaa years early – that wis odd.
G. They wanted him oot o his cell
Tae get it ready for Ken Dodd.

S. George Bush elected President;
(Ronald) Reagan's ready to quit.
B. With Dan Quayle waiting in the wings
We hope George Bush keeps fit.
G. But here's the final headline
S. Being discussed in all the pubs –
B. Rangers are banned from Europe
All. Like all the other English clubs.

Ken Dodd: In the event Ken was found not guilty of swicking the tax man, to the great delight of the citizenry of Knotty Ash (twinned with Auchterturra).

Three Tenors

P.A. Announcement: And now for the first time in Scotland please welcome the world's three greatest tenors, José Carreras, Placido Domingo and Luciano Pavarotti.

La Donna E Mobile

Hoots mon,
Hoch aye
The noo,
We've come to sing to you.
Hail-a Caledonia
From the land of macaroni-a.
We're the kings of melody,
As good as Calum Kennedy.
You're talking through your hat –
We're not as good as that.
Very true,
But we do
Have a large repertoire.
And since we're
Singing here
We'll sing to you the songs o Scotland.

Auld Scots Sangs

We'll sing tae you the new Scots sangs,
The tunes are far from done;
The words seem strange,
But they've got to change
For 1991.

Road to the Isles

There's a tunnel 'neath the Chunnel
That joins England on tae France
And the roads in Kent are clogging up for miles.
So if you live in Scotland
And you want to go to France
You'd be quicker going by the Road to the Isles.

Grannie's Heiland Hame

There's a dump for nuclear rubbish
Jist ootside Grannie's door.
How mony heids has your cat got?
'Cos Grannie's cat's got four.

The Piper o Dundee

A paper comes tae oor toon,
Tae your toon,
Tae every toon;
An Scottish folk fae Wick tae Troon
They read it greedily.
It's D C Thomson's constant boast
That paper's read fae coast tae coast.
Let's hear it for the *Sunday Post,*
The paper o Dundee.

Comin Through The Rye

Gie's a Bloody Mary, laddie,
God! I'm bloody dry
Let's get blotto, that's my motto
Quick – before I die.
Large Glendronnach, gin and tonic –
Are these elephants pink?
Rum or Brandy; ev'n a Shandy
'S long as it's a drink;
Best champagne or
Something plainer,
What else can I try?
Give's that bottle of Yankee stuff,
And I'll get through the rye.

The Northern Lights

The Northern Line to Old Aberdeen
From Edinbro via Dundee –
The trains aren't packed, they're on time and they're clean.
You tak different trains fae me.

Few things are certain in this life,
But I'm sure deep down inside
The Northern Line to Aberdeen
Won't be electrified.

A Gordon For Me

The Gordons, dear me,
Are merging, I see,
As part of some crazy defence strategy.
Their record is braw,
Their recruitment an aa,
So to cock up the Gordons maks nae sense at aa.

Annie Laurie

Big Robert Maxwell wis nae too bonny,
The 22-stone clown,
He swore he'd go down in history,
Well, he certainly went down.
But where's the pension fund
Of a hundred million quid?
Though folk say that you can't take it with you,
Ye get the feeling Maxwell did.

Loch Lomond

A lot o folk are pushin
For Scottish devolution,
And total independence micht suit us;
But picture Major's face
If ever that took place
'Cos England wid be up the creek withoot us.

Westering Home

In the Western Isles morale isn't high,
Since the Council invested with BCCI.
So there's nothing for breakfast, there's nothing to fry
Since they put all their eggs in one basket.

(In 1995 lines 3 and 4 were altered to:)

But they learned their lesson, once bitten twice shy
They moved all their money to Barings.

The Deil's Awa wi the Exciseman

Gordon Brown, John Smith and Robin Cook
Are the stars of the Labour Party,
But Scots MPs aren't all like that –
Not every one is a smartie.
George Robertson looks saft,
Dennis Canavan's daft,
And what's obvious mair and mair is –
Dalzell's awa, Dalzell's awa, Dalzell's awa wi the fairies.

Figaro

We, Pavarotti, Carreras, Domingo are
Of contemp'rary singers the greatest.
We – will do gigs where we think that the big bucks are,
And this visit to Scotland's the latest.
We come expensive, though;
You'll never engage us,
Just think of our wages.
We're really pricey:
Caruso, he wus
Cheaper than us.

Though
We are artists of sensitivitee,
Still for money we really are gluttons.
So
When we come to discuss what our fee might be,
What's important's the number of nothin's.

Music'lly Mozart was good,
Nobody could
Say he was not;
But with the pounds and the pence
His business sense
Wasn't too hot:
He was a clot,
The pauper of opera, he came a cropper and
That was his lot.

But, pay attention,
May we just mention,
We've no intention
Of ending up poor.

Three singing gallants,
Magical talents,
And our bank balance
Proves it for sure.

So it is riches
To which we aspire,
So higher and higher
Our bank balance goes.

We give you flashy stuff,
None of your trashy stuff,
Like Pagliacci –
Classy but catchy.
The point of this stunt is –
Our aim, to be blunt, is
For thousands of punters
To pay through the nose.

When we negotiate,
Zeroes are what we rate,
We like a lot of those
Nice figure 0's.

Figure 0's, figure 0's
Figure 0's, figure 0's
We like a fee full of figure 0's.

The figure 0 is the figure that counts,
We like it: we like to see figure 0's in our fee.
Each little nought
Does mean a lot.
Each figure 0 that you add on the end –
The fee will increase by a factor of ten.

Figure 0's – say four,
Figure 0's – one more,
Figure 0 here, figure 0 there
Figure 0 wheett! out of the air,
Figure 0's nice – all in a row,
All adding up – see the fee grow.
All we are doing is making a buck,
Let's add another wee zero for luck.
Zero for luck, zero for luck,
All we are doing is making a buck.

Three famous tenors
With songs of Vienna –
A little Puccini,
A touch of Rossini,
Some fast Donizetti
With notes like confetti.
Luciano gets sweaty
And everyone cheers.

As to the hire of us,
People enquire of us
How costly we would be.
How big our fee would be.
One word of caution – it
Could be extortionate
I'd say we'd cost you an arm and a leg.

So if you want to engage
Pavarotti, Carreras, Domingo,
Pay us a living wage,
Just think of a number
And add a few figure 0's,
Make the fee bigger 'cos
If we can charge enough –
If the fee's large enough,
We will SING for you.

Three tenors: These were three middle-aged hopefuls who during the 1980s gave up their day jobs as opera singers to become three strolling players known collectively as 'La Scala the What?'

The M.O.T. Test

A country garage. A phone rings and is answered by the garage proprietor, Mr Bert Petrie (Steve).

P.   Easy Terms Motors. Bert Petrie here. Specialisin in new cars, nearly new cars, nae sae new cars, but maistly bangers. Oh, it's yersel, Mrs McClaverty. Aye, ye pit in yer car for its M.O.T. and its first service efter 50,000 miles. Oh, Mr McClaverty's on his wye roon, is he? Eh? Wait till I get this richt noo. Ye forgot tae tell him that he'd tae drive roon past an collect yer holiday outfits fae Pullar's o Perth. Oh, but I'm sorry, he winna get the car oot the day. Heh, heh, heh. He'll be lucky if he ever gets it oot. But nae problem: I'll easy gie im a lift tae Pullars. Oh, dinna thank me, I'm forever takkin folk tae the cleaners.

Enter Mr McClaverty (Buff)

McC.   Hello, Mr Petrie. Did my wife phone?

P.   Hello, Mr McClaverty. Aye, she phoned.

McC.   Sorry I'm late. I'd to pop in past the travel agent. We're off to France on Monday. A motoring holiday on the Continent.

P.   Ha, ha, ha, ha. No, no, no, Mr McClaverty. That car's nae gaan naewye. Nae in the state that it's in. No, no. I doot it's the bus oot tae Ballater for you.

McC.   But we've got the car booked on the motorail.

P.   Oh, it wid be aa richt on the motorail. Aat's the best place for it. 'Cos it'll never ging naewye itsel.

McC.   What?

P.   Well, I've jist hid the report through fae the workshop. An it disna mak good readin. (*The report comes through as a computer print-out – apparently never-ending.*) There's a lot o readin but it's nae good readin. Oh, me, aat's terrible aat.

McC.   What is it?

P.   The new foreman canna spell 'clapped oot'. Look, he gets it wrang every time. An here's anither een he canna spell: 'terminal'.

McC. There's something wrong with a terminal?

P. No. 'Terminal' is his final diagnosis.

McC. Look, I'm needing the car urgently. We're going to France on Monday.

P. Of course.

McC. And we can't go to France without a licence for the car. And we can't get a licence for the car unless you give me an MOT Certificate.

P. An I canna gie ye an MOT Certificate unless yer car's in a roadworthy condition. An yer car winna be in a roadworthy condition till we've deen twaa or three little thingies til't, an a hale heep o big eens.

McC. But we've paid for our holiday in advance.

P. Ye hinna, hiv ye? Hiv ye ever heard the expression: 'Pinted yersel intae a corner?'

McC. Look, you'd better tell me the worst.

P. Weel, it's hard tae say fit een is the worst. They're aa bad. Bit I'll jist ging through it wi ye. Excuse me if I get a bittie technical. Right. Yer steerin wheel's shoogly. Yer cam-shaft's noisy, an yer cylinder gasket's knackered. Ye see, aat's aa bad news.

McC. So why is the car running so smoothly?

P. 'Cos yer tyres is bald. And here's anither een – yer coolin system's sufferin fae severe oxidisation.

McC. What does that mean?

P. Yer radiator's roosty and requires replacement.

McC. Come on, you don't replace every rusty radiator.

P. But you're a special case, Mr McClaverty. You're desperate. I've got you by the short an . . . I've got your interests at heart.

McC. Thanks very much. What else does it say?

P. Weel, ye're sufferin fae piston slap, yer Hardy Spicer's gone, yer crank shaft's connached, yer windscreen wipers is wonky, yer big end's went, an yer brakes is buggered. God, he canna even spell 'buggered'. He should've used a shorter word.

McC. What's all this work going to cost?

P. Weel, put it this wye. Ye could be lookin at a fair bit o money here.

McC. But how much? Can you give me a ball-park figure?

P. Weel, it's mair a golf course figure.

McC. That's a lot worse than I expected.

P. I ken. Ye ken the best answer for you? Get yersel a new car.

McC. A new car?

P. I've got a hale showroom full o new cars aa dyin tae ging tae France for their holidays. An I mean, aat aal banger o yours, trade it in. It's deen . . finished . . . had its day. Shot its bolt.

McC. I suppose so. What you're saying is – you can't put back the clock.

P. You can't put back the clock. Spik for yersel.

McC. Well, it's a big decision. I mean, is there anything right about that car at all?

P. There's naething wrang wi the noddin dog in the back windae.

Ballater: Home of the famous toy shop (see vol. 1, p. 131) where the Princess of Wales purchased a cuddly futret and two rubber ducks. Could it have been this experience which made her famously hostile to Upper Deeside, or was there perhaps something else?

The Edinburgh Smell

There is some-thing in the air, Some-thing no-bo-dy can miss. Peo-ple sense it ev-ry where. What strange mys-ter-y is this? It's like no-thing else I know, It's in-clined to come and go. I think that I can feel it com-ing on. Oh what is this u-nique phe-nom-e-non? It's the Ed-in-burgh smell that is weav-ing its spell And its source can be eas-i-ly traced. The ar-o-ma's re-leased from a fer-ment of yeast with a whiff of in-

dus - tri - al waste. And the'n - vir - on - men - tal cost of a

thou - sand ex - hausts Means there's car - bon - di - ox - ide as well

Put all these to - geth - er and with the right wea - ther you

get the most glor - i - ous smell. The glor - i - ous

Ed - in - burgh smell.

There is something in the air,
Something nobody can miss,
People sense it everywhere,
What strange mystery is this?
It's like nothing else I know,
It's inclined to come and go;
I think that I can feel it comin on –
What is this unique phenomenon?

It's the Edinburgh smell that is weaving its spell,
And its source can be easily traced.
The aroma's released from a ferment of yeast
With a whiff of industrial waste.
And the environmental costs of a thousand exhausts
Means there's carbon monoxide as well.
Put all these together and with the right weather
You get the most glorious smell (*repeat*).

If you're Edinbro bound and there's fog on the ground,
Or you're blinded by blizzards or snows,
Not a sign of a light, but you get there all right,
You just have to follow your nose.
That odour has shown it's a will of its own,
It's been known to go many a mile.
When the wind's in the north and blows up off the Forth,
Then the smell often reaches Carlisle (*repeat*)

For the ultimate purist, the Japanese tourist,
Edinbro has so much to give.
Attractions abound – Princes Street and the Mound
And the house where John Knox used to live.
The Castle's prodigious, and two great Forth Bridges,
And the price at the Caley Hotel;
When the visitor goes, he forgets all of those,
But he'll always remember the smell (*repeat*).

Sean Connery will tell he grew up with the smell,
(He's local, as everyone knows)
Till one fateful day he said, 'Och, I'm away,
That smell really gets up my nose.'
He'd have stayed with his old man – he'd still be a coalman,
That smell made young Connery rebel.
Now in films he's a figure than whom there's none bigger,
He owes all of that to the smell (*repeat*).

That smell is so great it, should be celebrated,
Let's up to the rooftops and shout.
It's the Edinbro pong, not the Pont d'Avignon
That songs should be written about.
It's now understood that around Hollyrood
Is a pricy location to dwell.
Living near to the yeast your poll-tax is increased,
Well, you're getting the best of the smell.

It's right you should pay,
'Cos just smell that bouquet
Oh, you're getting the best of the smell.
Oh, the reek in Auld Reekie
Is kinda uniquie –
Three cheers for the Edinburgh smell!

Nona's Knickers

(Tune: Donald, Whaur's Yer Troosers?)

Buff: (*Addressing the audience*) Very recently Andy Stewart had a big hit with a revival of 'Donald, Whaur's Yer Troosers?' At about the same time that other great Scottish entertainer, Ron Brown MP, also had a hit in the flat of his research assistant, Nona. In fact it wasn't just a hit, it was a smash, and in the course of it Nona lost two pairs of – how shall I put it? – two items of underwear.

If Andy had known this story, he wouldn't have been asking Donald where his troosers were – he'd have been asking something else. Ladies and gentlemen, Andy Stewart. Enter Andy (Steve), who sings:

This is the tale of the great Ron Brown,
Scotland's Parliamentary clown,
And his cry that ran through London Town –
'Nona, whaur's yer knickers?'

A fetishistic fellow was he,
Heavily intae lingerie;
Hence poor Ron's impassioned plea:
'Nona, whaur's yer knickers?'

Nona was Ron's researcher fair,
Ron researched her underwear,
Offering up this plaintive prayer:
'Nona, whaur's yer knickers?'

He visited most of Brighton's bars
And after a bevy of a good few jars
He was after Nona's directoires,
Shoutin, 'Nona, whaur's yer knickers?'

Oh, Ron searched high and Ron searched low;
Through her flat like a tor-na-do
Went that knicker-fixated Romeo
Cryin, 'Nona, whaur's yer knickers?'

Ron in that flat went over the top
In the words of one hard-bitten cop:
'He was like a bull in a china shop
Lookin for Nona's knickers.'

After a frantic, frenzied blitz
(Mirrors and plates in a million bits)
The Hon'rable Member for Leith just sits
Cryin, 'Nona, whaur's yer knickers?'

He'd wrecked her wardrobe with great force
(A genuine imitation Louis Quatorze)
Then it dawned on Ron that the chest of draw'rs
Was the place she'd keep her knickers.

His face went red, his face went blue,
As Ron that chest of drawers went through,
Then he came across not one but two
Pairs of Nona's knickers.

When Nona came home her flat was wrecked
So all her personal things she checked,
Till she suddenly asked herself direct
'Whaur the hell's my knickers?'

(They were) the only knickers that Nona possessed
Since then she's never been fully dressed;
On the tennis court her opponents protest,
'Hey, Nona, whaur's yer knickers?'

At the trial of Ron the learned judge
Said, 'I'd like to see these knickers', nudge, nudge.
Well, you see, he was a Scottish Judge,
And he fancied Nona's knickers.

Louis Quatorze: King of France (1643-1715) and cabinet-maker, though he didn't need a cabinet, being an absolute monarch much given to saying, 'L'état c'est moi,' an expression frequently used, as it happens, by Ron Brown, on whose lips however it usually means 'Oh me, fit a state I'm in.'

I Know the Face

George: (*Addressing the audience.*) See these two chaps. There's Bill. And there's Roddy. They're at a party and they are just about to meet. Bill (Buff) knows everything about Roddy (Steve). As for Roddy – he knows the face but, well – you know the embarrassing feeling.

B.   (*Addressing an unseen guest.*) Sorry to interrupt, but I just spotted Roddy Balfour over there. (*Waves.*)

R.   (*Addressing another unseen guest.*) Who's that chap giving me the wave? I know the face, but what the hell's his name? I do hope he doesn't come over and speak to me.

B.   I must go over and speak to him. (*Approaches and shakes hands with Roddy.*) Well, well, well – hello Roddy.

R.   Well, well, well – hello – there.

B.   It's – Roddy Balfour.

R.   It's – nice to see you.

B.   How's Mabel?

R.   Fine. Fine. How's – your own good lady?

B.   Oh fine, fine, fine. Veronica's fine.

R.   Veronica. That's fine, fine.

B.   And how are those two youngsters of yours?

R.   Fine, fine.

B.   Alan still enjoying the Air Force?

R.   Fine, fine.

B.   And Louise?

R.   Fine, fine.

B.   Now, let's see – Louise must be in her third year at Heriot Watt.

R. Yes, yes.

B. You know, I think it's great the way Alan and Louise have always got on well with my lot.

R. Great. Great. Terrific. And how are – your lot?

B. Fine, fine, fine.

R. Do forgive me – I get a wee bit mixed up about what your lot are doing at the moment.

B. Well, which one are you interested in?

R. Which one am I not interested in?

B. Well, let's talk about the oldest – let's talk about Leslie.

R. Leslie – the oldest! How's Leslie?

B. Well Leslie goes from strength to strength.

R. Leslie goes from strength to strength. Isn't that terrific!

B. Well, you know our Leslie . . .

R. Your Leslie is quite a character. You know. Forgive me, but Mabel and I sometimes wonder when you and Verandah – eh – Veronica called Leslie, Leslie, were you not just a wee bit worried that Leslie's both a boy's name and a girl's name?

B. Maybe we should have – but och – it never occurred to us. And it's worked out fine. Well, I don't need to tell you that there's no mistaking our Leslie!

R. Uhhh, No, no . . .

B. So that's Leslie.

R. That's Leslie – that's Leslie . . . good old Leslie. And how about – number two?

B. Pat.

R. Pat! How's Pat?

B. Pat's fine.

R. Pat's fine.

B. Pat's fine. Of course, Pat's in America.

R. Pat's in America!

B. Aye.

R. Pat's in America!

B. Pat's in America. Well, you know America – young man's country . . . and a young woman's country. Pat's getting married out there.

R. Oh great! And who's the lucky . . . American?

B. Well, not a particularly American name – Robinson.

R. Robinson.

B. Francis Robinson

R. Pat's marrying Francis?

B. Right.

R. Oh, I hope they'll be very happy together.

B. So that's Leslie, and Pat, and last but not least . . . the twins.

R. The twins?

B. Both teaching now.

R. Oh, they're not that age already.

B. Aye, Jackie and Lindsay. Here, how are you getting on in your new house?

R. Fine.

B. Now, let's see – what is it? 73 Orchard Road?

R. Yes, yes.

B. Two along from the corner, beside the pillar box, roses in the front – lovely yellow roses.

R. Are they not pink?

B. Yes, they're pink. What a dreadful memory I've got!

R. I could have sworn they were pink. And are you still in . . . the same neck of the woods?

B. No, no, no – we've moved out to Cults.

R. Cults! Yes, I think I did hear that. Yes, Mabel bumped into Verucca – eh, Veronica. At the chiropodists I think it was. Do you like Cults – better than . . . where you were?

B. Where we were?

R. Nearer the centre of things.

B. Och well, it wasn't that much of a move, after all. I mean, we were at the extreme end of Mannofield.

R. Mannofield! Yes, well, if you're going to move to Cults, Mannofield's the place to move from. I mean you couldn't get an easier place to move to Cults from than Mannofield. Particularly the extreme end.

B. So that's what – about six months you've been in Orchard Road?

R. Yes! Yes.

B. Mabel getting used to the eye level grill?

R. Yes. Yes.

B. Mabel's mum still with you?

R. Yes, getting on, eighty-seven now, of course, you know.

B. I thought she was eighty-eight?

R. God, that's right. She had a birthday last week . . . !

B. I was going to say – good picture of you in the evening paper last week.

R. Which one was that?

B. The one at the opening of the new sewage works.

R. There was one at the Engineers' Dinner too.

B. I saw that one too – but, no, no it was the one at the opening of the new sewage works. I was just thinking, that must be the biggest project you've been involved in . . .

R. Mmmm. I suppose it is.

B. . . . in thirty-six years with the Council.

R. Is it thirty-six years? Oh well, you would know. How are your own waterworks? How's your own . . . work?

B. Well you know – toiling in the same old vineyard.

R. Vineyard! Ploughing an honest furrow.

B. Getting through the day's darg.

114

R. I hope your're reaping a few of the fruits . . . of your labours . . . whatever they are!

B. Well, earning a crust you know, earning a crust. Our big problem is getting supplies.

R. Supplies. Yes. Well supplies would be a problem. Supplies, a problem. Oh yes, yes, yes. Oh well, at least supplies are never a problem at the sewage work.

B. Talking of which . . . have you heard old Harry Wilson's up to his neck in the you know what?

R. Dear me no. Oh I'm sorry to hear that. Who's Harry Wilson?

B. The chap you were speaking to when I came over.

R. Was that . . . Harry Wilson?

B. Aye . . .

R. It was so embarrassing, you know. This chap came up to speak to me – I knew the face but could I remember his name!

B. Well, I could see you were struggling, so I thought I'd come over and rescue you.

You couldn't get an easier place to move to Cults from than Mannofield: Well, you could, actually; because Pitfodels lies between them. But we hope this minor solecism didn't spoil anyone's enjoyment of the sketch.

The Census

Our life-style here in the land of the free Is com-pared with some at-trac-tive, There's just one thing that both-ers me Big Broth-er's al-ways ac-tive, And on Ap-ril twen-ty-first this year Big Bro-ther held a cen-sus here Now stored in a com-put-er with a dat-a-base is ev'-ry sin-gle fact a-bout the pop-u-lace.

Rall..

What a lot of ques- tions the Cen- sus asked What a lot of in- fo

was a- massed all a -bout your pre- sent and your past And it's

all gone in- to the da- ta- base. Lots of forms com- plet- ed with

out a grouse How man- y bed- rooms in your house? Are

you still sleep- ing with your spouse? It's all gone in- to the

da- ta- base. What a- bout your ed- u- ca- tion

117

Spec - i - fy each qual - i - fic - a - tion Were you bright at school or rot - ten Or like John Ma - jor have you for - got - ten No look - ing blank no sav - ing face That must go in - to the dat - a - base.

End of last verse

'Cos mark my word It' ll be ig - nored All the da - ta that's stored in the da - ta - base.

L.H.

21st April '91
And a difficult duty to be done,
And you had to be conscientious
When you were filling in your census.
Now every detail of the populace
Is stored in one big data base.

What a lot of questions the census asked,
What a lot of info was amassed,
All about your present and your past,
And it's all gone into the data base.

Forms filled in without a grouse
How many bedrooms in your house?
Are you still sleeping with your spouse?
It's all gone into the data base.

What about your education?
Specify each qualification
Were you bright at school or rotten?
Or, like John Major, have forgotten?
No looking blank, no saving face,
That must go into the data base.

List those living at your flat,
Reveal to the faceless bureaucrat
The ethnic origin of your cat;
It all goes into the data base.

What was your job in '61?
Have you ever had a vasectomy done?
(Women are allowed to ignore that one)
But it all goes into the data base.

This one's got me in a pickle:
'Do you own a motor or other vehicle?'
Well, I've two cars – what could be sadder?
One's a wreck and the other's a Lada.
Each of them is a hopeless case,
But they both go into the data base.

Where d'you go to do your job?
Has your front door got a big brass knob?
Has your whatsit got a thingummy-bob?
It all goes into the data base.

The type of house that you live in,
The colour and size of your rubbish bin,
The name, age and sex of your bidie-in,
It's all gone into the data base.

What you answer for the census
All in strictest confidence is.
Not for a hundred years will the neighbours
Ascertain the outcome of these labours.
So do be frank; fear no disgrace,
Your secrets are safe in the data base.

I suppose these things there's a need to know,
Like what's the size of your sewage outflow?
And where does all that sewage go?
It all goes into the data base.

And what's the purpose of this task?
That's one thing they forgot to ask,
And no amount of flannel can mask
That they haven't a clue
What the hell to do
With the data they can view
In the data base.

John Major: Prime Minister of Great Britain since 1990, but seems longer; at the time of going to print, jist hingin on by one vote, his fingernails and the grace of God. The reference is to his feat of restoring national confidence, as soon as he came to power, by forgetting how many O-levels he had obtained.

How About You?

I like Scotland, though it's small – how about you?
I like it, warts and all – how about you?
I even like Forsyth, Graeme Souness too,
I like Stranraer in May, Sunday in Stornoway,
How about you?
That scowl of Robin Cook's
Can't put me off him,
Nor Donald Dewar's looks –
Though they're equally grim.
Muriel Gray leaves me unimpressed,
And Rab C Nesbitt's vest
May not be new,
But I like it, how about you?

I like Coatbridge in June – how about you?
Taggart and Daphne Broon – how about you?
I worship *Evening Call*, *Take the High Road* too,
I like the Bathgate air, Archie McPherson's hair,
How about you?
I've always liked John Knox – he liked a good time;
And Nicky Fairbairn's frocks are really sublime
Neeps and Haggis with mushy peas –
Pass the Alkaseltzer, please,
Dyspepsia's due,
But I like it, how about you?

I like Kirkcaldy's smell – how about you?
I like Cowdenbeath as well – how about you?
I like a Scotrail train when it's overdue,
I'd welcome Tom and Jack, the Alexander Brothers, back –
How about you?
I like the Glesca Fair, I like Hogmanay,
I like the fine clear air up round Dounereay.
Every daft Regional Council scheme,
All the Scots in the Rangers team –
I've counted two
But I like it here, how about –
I can't see me getting out
I like it here, how about
You?

Closing Reprise

G.   I like a bagpipe tune – how about you?

B.   Aye, if the sound's turned doon – how about you?

S.   I do like Ian Lang, and the plum in his moo.

G.   I like to speculate on Magnus Magnusson's sell-by date.
How about you?

B.   I give Edinbro ten out of ten.
Of cities a star;

S.   I like it even when
I'm parking a car

G.   Scots hotels can be quite bizarre –

B.   Threatening to close the bar,

S.   And they frequently do,

All.   So we're going, how about –
If you're quick now, you'll get out
We're going, how about
You?
Good-night.

School Chums

The departure lounge of Aberdeen Airport, where a scruffy man, Stewart Strachan (Steve) is seated.

P.A. British Airways announce the departure of Flight BA523 for London, Heathrow. Passengers for this flight should make their way to the Departure Lounge.

Enter a smart, confident man, Gordon Ogilvie (Buff) carrying the Financial Times. He sits down beside Stewart.

S. It's Gordon, isn't it? Gogs. Gogs Ogilvie. We wis at the school thegither. Auchterturra Primary. Droopydrawers Davidson's class.

G. Hud on. Faa hiv we got here? God, it's Stushie Strachan.

S. Aat's richt. Stushie Strachan.

G. I can see ye yet. Ye aye sat in the very front seat aside Jeannie Sinclair. Mind? Wi the glae ee an the big nose.

S. Aat's richt.

G. An you were aye pingin her elastic.

S. Ha! Ha!

G. Mind you, faa didna dae that? Fit a dame she wis. She'd hiv gone roon the back o the cycle shed wi onybody for half o their play-time piece.

S. Aye. Ha! Ha!

G. Fit ever happened tae Jeannie?

S. I merried her.

G. Weel, aat wis good o ye.

S. I'd nae option.

G. Weel, weel. Stushie Strachan. How's the world been treatin ye, Stushie? Are ye managin tae mak a bob or twaa?

S. Weel, a bob or twaa's aboot the size o't. In a good wik.

G. I mind fan you left the school – I'm spikkin aboot thirty-five years ago, Stushie – ye said ye were gaan awaa intae Aiberdeen tae seek yer fortune.

S. Aat's richt. Weel, I wis lucky enough tae get a job my very first day.

G. Oh, that wis lucky. Fit did ye get?

S. I got a post wi a big fish processin business.

G. Oh, aye. Were ye a management trainee?

S. No.

G. Wis ye on the sales side?

S. No.

G. Wis ye a buyer?

S.   No.

G.   A filleter?

S.   No.

G.   Fit did ye dae?

S.   I swept the fleer in the fish hoose. But fit aboot yersel, Gogs? Fit hiv you been daein? Faa did you mairry?

G.   I finished up wi Maisie Middleton. Ye'll maybe mind her. She wis Miss Scotland three years runnin.

S.   Oh, very nice. Fit Middleton wis aat noo?

G.   Middleton the haulage contractor.

S.   Did she drive a larry?

G.   No, her aal man wis the haulage contractor.

S.   Oh, aye. Aal Middleton – he'd larries aa wye. He wis worth a fortune, aal Middleton. Fit happened til im?

G.   He dee'd. It wis affa sudden. An Maisie bein the only child I wis kinda trapped. I'd nae option but tae tak ower a business worth ten million quid.

S.   Oh, fit a shame.

G.   So I selt oot, for a hunner million.

S.   Oh, aat's a bittie better.

G.   Aye, an American boy cam in aboot, an that wis his offer. Weel, I didna ken naething aboot larries, but it didna seem too bad.

S.   Weel, aat *wisna* too bad, Gogs. A hunner million.

G.   Aye, nae pounds, jist dollars.

S.   Oh, jist dollars. Oh't a shame. Mind you, a hunner million dollars, it's still better than a slap in the belly wi a weet huddock. An I'm spikkin fae experience, Gogs.

G. Aye. Tell me mair aboot yer career in the fish trade. Ye started sweepin the fleer in the fish hoose.

S. Aye, weel, somebody had tae dae't. 'Cos fit a mess it wis, aat fleer. I think it wis the fish heids that wis the worst. I didna like the wye they looked at ye. I mean, ye can only dae a job like aat for sae lang, so I left.

G. Fan wis aat?

S. Last wik. The fish trade's gaan through a bad time. I wis made redundant.

G. Ye'd got a golden handshake, did ye?

S. I didna even get a golden cutlet.

G. An foo did Jeannie tak it?

S. Weel, ye ken this, Gogs? It made nae difference tae Jeannie at aa. She'd walked oot on me twenty years ago.

G. Twenty years ago? 1971? Aat wis a bad year for me an aa. Aat wis the year the aal man dee'd.

S. Oh, I'm sorry. I didna ken he wis ill.

G. Aye.

S. Ye'd been real close til im, wis ye, Gogs?

G. Aye, Stushie. Very close.

S. How close were ye, Gogs?

G. Weel, fan yer aal man's a multi-millionaire, ye never let him oot o yer sicht.

S. Of course, your faither wis aal Charlie Ogilvie, wisn't he? Charlie Ogilvie o Bailliesprotts.

G. Bailliesprotts, aye that's the hame ferm – wi the big hoose far me an Maisie bide noo. An we've a dizzen ithers that we work wirsels an anither dizzen that we let oot.

S. Yer aal man left ye aa that?

G. Aye, an nae jist that. There's the salmon fishin on the Dee, an aa his stocks an shares, an the grouse moor, an he'd a yacht doon aboot Mont –

S. Montrose?

G. Monte Carlo.

S. Mercy me, you inherited aa that? An there's nae brithers or sisters tae share the responsibility wi ye?

G. Naebody. The hale burden fell on my shouders.

S. Fit a shame.

G. Aye, it's nae easy, ye ken, Stushie. I mean, hiv ye ever had tae collect rent fae a bunch o thrawn tenant fermers?

S. Weel, no. But I ken fit ye mean, Gogs. Fan I wis in the fish hoose, I had tae collect the tea money. Ho! Ho! Fit a job that wis. Some o that fish quines – the language!

G. So tell me. Fit happened efter Jeannie left ye?

S. Weel, I'll tell ye. It wis an excitin time. The pressure wis really on. She left me wi the fower bairns tae bring up, an a heap o debt – hire purchase aa ower the place. Fit a challenge it wis. Some wiks I jist hid enough money tae buy a fish finger for the tea.

G. A fish finger's real fine for yer tea.

S. Nae fan there's jist een atween the five o's.

G. Weel, Stushie. Life certainly hisna been dull for ye. Ye're a lucky man.

S. Oh, I'm lucky. And I've come through. I've a wee place o my ain noo.

G. Oh? Faar aboot?

S. I've got my ain cubicle in the Salvation Army hostel.

G. Tell me, Stushie. Hiv ye ony plans for holidays this year?

S. No, I thocht I wid jist bide at hame an save up tae get my left shoe repaired. Fit aboot yersel? Hiv you anything fixed up?

G. Weel, we usually ging tae Mustique. But Maisie's taen an affa scunner at Princess Margaret. It's aa that smokin an drinkin.

S. It sounds jist like the Salvation Army hostel.

G. So this year we're slummin it on the QE2. It's the world cruise. Wi stop-overs at Singapore, Sydney an San Francisco.

S. Oh, a kinda days here and there?

G. So in three months' time, Stushie, ye can picter me sittin in my state-room on the QE2 thinkin tae mysel 'I'd raither be here than sweepin the fleer in an Aiberdeen fish hoose.' Excuse me for bein nosey, Stushie, but there's something botherin me. Fit wye can you afford tae ging tae London?

S. I canna. My daughter's sendin me my fare. She bides doon there an I hinna seen her for a whilie.

G. Weel, that's a coincidence. I've got a daughter in London.

S. Oh, fit dis she dae?

G. She's a solicitor roon aboot Lincoln's Inn.

S. Weel, that is a coincidence. My daughter's solicitin roon aboot King's Cross.

G. So faar'll ye be bidin in London?

S. Nae problem. I've got a reciprocal arrangement wi the Salvation Army hostel doon there. Fit aboot yersel?

G. Weel, I usually jist bide at my club.

S. Fit club's aat, noo?

G. The Carlton Club. It's men only. But ye get yer dinner, an if ye're stuck, a bed for the nicht.

S. It's exactly like the Salvation Army Hostel. So fit are you gaan tae London for?

G. I've an ICI Board Meetin in the mornin, and in the efterneen I'm pickin up my Knighthood.

128

S. Yer Knighthood? Very nice. So ye're gaan tae be Sir Gordon. Fit did ye get yer Knighthood for?

G. Services tae charity.

S. Charity?

G. Aye. Ye see, Stushie, I've got mair money than I ken fit tae dae wi.

S. Oh?

G. Aye. I've ower much money.

S. Oh fit a shame.

G. So I gie a lot o it awaa.

S. Oh, ye div?

G. Aye, If I can find a deservin cause. And I've found een the day, Stushie.

S. Oh, ye hiv?

G. Aye. I've met an aal school freen smilin in the face o adversity, an I'm gaan tae mak sure you've got a roof ower yer heid for the rest o yer days. I'm gaan tae write oot a cheque for a hunner thoosand quid.

S. Lovely.

G. Made payable tae the Salvation Army.

Roon the back o the cycle shed: This was where Stushie and Jeannie (like many others) began their relationship before graduating in due course to Lovers' Lane and thereafter to Bonkers' Neuk (a name which in the 1990s superseded its previous, less felicitous, designation.) See map of Auchterturra on endpapers.

I'd nae option: Visits to Bonkers' Neuk were inclined to have the effect of restricting young men's options.

Junk Mail

Junk mail, junk mail,
It's increasing in scale . . .

What do you do with your junk mail
When you get it in the morning?
Like a load of rocks through the letter box
There's junk mail every morning.
Here's the offer of a prize quite remarkable in size –
Is your rule to chuck it out without a look?
Here's a pamphlet testifying *Readers' Digest* is worth buying
If you're not quite at the stage to read a book.

What's at the top of your junk mail?
Well, the big hard sell is time-share.
Yes, the commonest of late is the tempting bait
To seduce you into time-share.
Could you see yourself sign on the dotted line?
Here's a plausible brochure that says you should,
But if you're thinking of investing, can it really be suggesting
That the fourth week in November would be good?

What do you do when your junk mail
Contains something offensive?
Well, to be precise, it is not very nice
To receive something offensive.
It makes you really mad when the targetting is bad –
They should think of who the stuff's directed at;
When a sleazy firm in London sends a catalogue of condoms,
What does Maiden Aunt Jemima make of that?

Junk mail, junk mail,
It's increasing in scale . . .

Loads of paper –
What a caper,
All comprising
Advertising:
Fast maturing
Life insurance,
Time-share villas,
Cheap weed-killers;

Harvey Nichols,
Branston Pickles,
Slimming courses,
Quick divorces;
Garden centre
Impedimenta,
Luxury cruises,
Home jacuzzis;

Glazing (double) –
Loads of trouble;
Fire alarms.
Fitness farms,
Lots of hideous
Nasty videos,
Really tedious
Encyclopedias –

It's an endless tale,
And it's all junk mail . . .

What is it made from, your junk mail
And everybody else's?
What is the source of mine and of yours
And everybody else's?
Well the cost, if you please,
Must be counted in trees:
From the Amazon there's tales of dwindling stocks;
There's a mercen'ry Brazilian
Who has cut down several million,
And they end up dropping through your letter box.

If I was a tree I would hate junk mail
'Cos they'd chop down me to create junk mail.
It's become a lot more than a pest, junk mail.
A lot of people do detest junk mail –
Well, it's making me girnier and girnier,
Because I am a postie with a hernia.

The Insurance Policy

The Bar in a Golf Club-House. Hector (Steve), a Bar-Fly is seated at the Bar. Enter Bill (Buff) who sits down beside him.

B.   Hello, Hector.

H.   Hello, old boy. Have you been round?

B.   Aye. Just finished. It was the Insurance Golf Outing this morning.

H.   Insurance! I always thought you were one of those tooth-pullers?

B.   No, it's my twin brother who's the dentist.

H.   Do you ever come into the club with your twin brother?

B.   Aye. Quite often.

H.   Thank God for that. I sometimes think I'm seeing double.

B.   Actually, I'd like you to meet my twin brother.

H.   (*Looking at the empty space beside Bill.*) How do you do? I'm so pleased to meet you. Insurance, eh?

B.   Aye.

H.   Life insurance?

B.   Mainly.

H.   I had a life insurance once.

B.   Not any more?

H.   No. Cashed it in. Had to keep the old ship afloat. Going through a bad patch. 1952-1986. Then the old man kicked the bucket. God, that was a life-saver.

B.   So are you saying you haven't got any life cover at all?

H.   That's about the size of it.

B.   Well, you're taking a helluva chance. And what about Cathy? You see, you

could have a mutual policy, and if Cathy went first, you would benefit.

H. You mean if Cathy popped off, I'd get money as well? Talk about the icing on the cake. Have you got a form on you?

B. Well, I do just happen to have a proposal form in the hip pocket of my golfing trousers. No commitment or obligation, till after you've signed. Now, your name and – I can fill that in myself. Occupation?

H. Company Director. Fish merchant.

B. Who owns the business? Is it you?

H. Me and the Clydesdale Bank.

B. Was it your father who started the business?

H. That's right. The old man built it up. I've scaled it down a bit. Just me and the cashier now. And she does a bit of gutting on a Friday.

B. I get the picture. Now, Part 2 – your Medical History. Question 1. When did you last see your doctor?

H. Closing time yesterday. It was in here. That's his seat. He's late on parade this morning. Or you wouldn't have got that seat. Your brother would be all right. (*To empty space.*) You'd be alright, old boy.

B. Question 2. Other members of the proposer's family. How old was your father when he died?

H. Eighty-six.

B. Well, that's good, you see. He died playing golf here, didn't he?

H. That's right. Snuffed it on the seventh green. Rotten luck. He'd just holed a long putt.

B. He was playing with Tommy Calder, wasn't he?

H. Yes. Tommy was terribly upset.

B. So it was Tommy who reported it?

H. As soon as he finished his round.

B. What?

H. Well, after he'd had a couple of drinks in here.

B. And you've an older brother, haven't you?

H. That's right, Gerald.

B. That's funny. My brother's name is Gerald.

H. What? This one here? (*To empty space.*) Is your name Gerald? What a coincidence.

B. Your Gerald went off to Saudi Arabia, didn't he?

H. That's right. He's getting fifty lashes next week. I told him it was the wrong place to open a pub.

B. Now, epilepsy or paralysis. Well, you've never been epileptic?

H. Epileptic no. Paralytic frequently.

B.   Any complaints relating to bowels or bladder?

H.   Bowels or bladder?

B.   Your bladder. No complaints about it?

H.   Only from a bus driver once. On the way home from a golf outing.

B.   I heard about that. It was the Club outing to St Andrews. And on the way home you had to stop the bus five times.

H.   Between St Andrews and Dundee.

B.   Have you lived outside the UK in the past five years?

H.   I'm sorry?

B.   What they're getting at in this one is – have you ever been away from civilisation?

H.   Had to go to Edinburgh once.

B.   Oh, I think we'd count Edinburgh as civilised.

H.   You've never been in Rose Street during the General Assembly.

B.   Have you ever had an operation?

H.   No.

B.   X-Ray?

H.   No.

B.   Any special investigations?

H.   The VAT Inspector came in last week.

B.   Any amputations? Have you had anything cut off?

H.   Only the telephone.

B.   Ever had any broken bones?

H. Right hip. Lossiemouth. Northern Open 1983. Coming out of the hospitality tent. Fell on my hip flask.

B. Any trouble with your eyesight?

H. No. I can see you perfectly. And I can see Gerald perfectly too.

B. Well, that's about it. You won't regret this, Hector. This is linked to a wee accident policy. You get one thousand pounds if you lose a finger. Loss of hearing, you get five thousand pounds.

H. I'm sorry?

B. Lose one leg, you get ten thousand pounds. Lose both legs you get fifty thousand pounds.

H. That's the kind of policy for me. Loadsamoney for being legless.

Between St Andrews and Dundee: A primary school teacher who saw this sketch was reminded by this line of one of those old-fashioned proportion problems, viz:- 'A bus travels the thirteen miles between St Andrews and Dundee, and during that journey Hector has to get off the bus five times. How many times did Hector get off between Dundee and Aberdeen which are sixty-five miles apart?' The answer is 'none', because after the fifth stop a vote was taken on the bus and Hector wasn't allowed back on. Later that night he was seen lurching aboard the *Discovery* in search of a tot of rum.

In the hip pocket of my golfing trousers: All insurance agents do carry proposal forms in the hip pocket of their golfing trousers, or did, until one of them submitted a completed proposal form instead of his score card and had his handicap increased to twenty-eight.

Proud to be Scottish

You see here be - fore you three proud Scot - tish men. Sons of the land of the
moun - tain and glen. When talk - ing to strang - ers in pubs or in trains. The
blood of the Wall - ace pumps through our veins. But though we are burst - ing with
Nat - ion al pride. There are some of our count - ry - men we can't a - bide. I don't like the
le - gions of jok - ey Glas - weg - ians. But I'm proud that I am Scot - tish.
The Ed - in - bu - rgh folk are gey stiff like a pok - er. But I'm proud that

I am Scot - ish. And in Ai - ber - deen they're in - cred - ib - ly

mean. And there's ne - ver much glee in Dun - dee. And much worse than

last verse to Coda

these yins are the fly In - ver - nes - ians. But I'm proud that I am Scot - tish.

Coda

I we are

8ve

proud. Let's shout it a - loud We're proud that we

are Scot - tish.

We stand here before you, three proud Scottish men,
Sons of the land of the mountain and glen.
When talking to strangers in pubs or in trains
The blood of the Wallace pumps through our veins;
But though we are bursting with national pride
There are some of our countrymen we can't abide . . .

I don't like the legions
Of pushy Glaswegians,
But I'm proud that I am Scottish.
The Edinburgh folk are
Gey stiff – like a poker,
But I'm proud that I am Scottish.
And in Aiberdeen
They're incredibly mean,
And there's never much glee
In Dundee;
And much worse than these yins
Are the fly Invernessians,
But I'm proud that I am Scottish.

I ken folk in Methil,
And they're naething thpethil,
But I'm proud that I am Scottish.
They're prickly in Thurso
And in Wick even more so,
But I'm proud that I am Scottish.
They're snooty in Troon
And uncouth in Dunoon,
And snobb'ry runs high in Milngavie;
It's only the smokie
That makes Arbroath OK,
But I'm proud that I am Scottish.

The Perths, the Kirkcudbrights
Are swelling with hubris,
But I'm proud that I am Scottish.
And in Machrihanish
They're terribly clannish
But I'm proud that I am Scottish.
I'm not keen on Ayr –
There's no honest men there,
And they're coorser by far
In Stranraer.

In Shetland a brick wall –
And there's odd folk in Kirkwall,
But I'm proud that I am Scottish.

In Airdrie and Motherwell
Folk don't treat each other well,
But I'm proud that I am Scottish.
In Falkirk and Stirling
They cheat when they're curling,
But I'm proud that I am Scottish.
John o Groats makes you swear –
Folk are distant up there,
And the folk ower in Mull are richt dull;
In the Borders as well, so
Stuff Melrose, stuff Kelso,
But I'm proud that I am Scottish.

In short you can keep all
Those five million people,
But *we* are proud,
Let's shout it aloud,
We're proud that we are Scottish.

Police News

P.C. (Buff) Good evening and welcome to *Police News*, the programme in which we invite you, the viewer, to help us, the – (*Consults notes.*) Grampian Police.

First of all this week, Saxone's shoe shop have reported the theft of a boot. Normally they would not have bothered to report this incident, but this boot was at the back of the manager's Ford Granada. And he is particularly concerned because unfortunately the Ford Granada is still attached to it.

Mr William Davidson, an Inverurie pensioner, was robbed in his own home by two men who tied him to the fridge for two hours. Local police praised Mr Davidson for remaining cool throughout.

Senior citizens in the Bridge of Dee area of Aberdeen are advised to beware of a tall young man who has found a clever way of depriving them of their hard-earned savings. What makes him so persuasive is his soft, pleasant voice, his easy, familiar manner, his deceptive line of patter, and the fact that he carries a Kalashnikov rifle.

In Huntly last week a daring crime took place in the industrial premises of R B Farquhar, the Portakabin specialists, when two mobile retail units were illegally removed. Managing Director Mr Forbes Shand said, 'Heavens above, goodness gracious, two retail units stolen, that's the worst case of shop-liftin I've ever heard o.'

We are anxious to receive information about an incident near Peterhead yesterday when a Grampian Regional Council underground shelter, specially designed to withstand nuclear attack, was completely destroyed by vandals.

Yesterday in Elgin a police constable stopped a man who was walking an unmuzzled Rotweiler. When the constable enquired if the dog was covered by third party insurance, the owner replied, 'No, it hasn't learned to drive yet.'

Someone who can drive is former racing champion Jackie Stewart who yesterday clocked a time of 236 mph – on the A9, at which point he was overtaken by two caravans.

Next, I have to report that the play-time bell has been stolen from the School for the Deaf. The theft was noticed last week, but subsequent enquiries have established it took place in 1935.

Finally, a story with a happy ending: the missing parrot has been found.

Viewers may recall that last week I reported the disappearance of a rare South American parrot from the house of its owner, Miss Alice Christie, Bogs of Sharnydubs, Auchterturra. Well, I'm pleased to report tonight that the parrot has in fact been recaptured, and here is the parrot.

We see a gaudily coloured parrot on a perch. The P.C. approaches it.

Now this parrot – having lived for over seventy years in Auchterturra with Miss Christie – is the world's first Doric speaking parrot.

Parrot. Aye, aye, fit like? Aye, aye, fit like? Nae bad avaa. Aye chaavin awaa. Nae bad avaa. Aye chaavin awaa.

P.C. Thank you.

Parrot. Aye, aye, fit like etc. ad nauseum

P.C. I'm sure the viewers would like to know your name. Can you tell them?

Parrot. Nae bother at aa. Nae bother at aa. My name is Rover. My name is Rover. Rover the parrot. Rover the parrot.

P.C.   But Rover is usually a dog's name. Why did Miss Christie give you a dog's name?

Parrot. 'Cos she's blin as a bat. She's blin as a bat. An I dinna like er. I dinna like er. I dinna like Miss Christie. I dinna like Miss Christie. I do not like Miss Christie.

P.C.   Right, we'll note that point. Now I know Miss Christie has got other pets. Tell us about them.

Parrot. She's got a singin canary. A singin canary. Doh, ray, me, fa, so, lah, tee, doh. Cruising down the river.

P.C.   And what is the singing canary's name?

Parrot. Kermit. Kermit the singin canary. Kermit the singin canary.

P.C.   But Kermit is a frog's name. Why did Miss Christie give a singing canary a frog's name?

Parrot. 'Cos she's deif as a post. An I dinna like er. I dinna like Miss Christie. I do not like . . .

P.C.   We've been through all that.

Parrot. Kermit disna like Miss Christie. Kermit canna stick Miss Christie. An Kermit kens aboot aat kind o thing. Kermit's nae a bird-brain.

P.C.   What else has she got?

Parrot. She's got a tortoise. A tortoise.

P.C.   A tortoise?

Parrot. A tortoise. He's a fine chappy, the tortoise. Aabody likes the tortoise. The tortoise disna mind Miss Christie. He's got an affa thick skin, the tortoise.

P.C.   I hardly dare ask this. But what is the tortoise's name?

Parrot. Red Rum.

P.C.   Why does Miss Christie give a tortoise a race-horse's name?

Parrot. She's daft as a brush. An I dinna like er. She's a nesty aal wifie. She's a bitch! She's a bitch.

P.C. Now, for some reason folks, Miss Christie doesn't want to take Rover here back into her house.

Parrot. Get the Cruelty! Get the Cruelty!

P.C. So tonight I'm appealing for a new home for this loveable bird.

Parrot. Aw.

P.C. Now, Rover, is there anyone you would not want to go to?

Parrot. I dinna wint tae ging tae Bernard. I dinna wint tae ging tae that mannie Bernard.

P.C. You don't want to go to Bernard? Bernard who?

Parrot. Bernard Matthews. I'm nae gaan. I'm nae gaan tae that mannie Bernard. I'm nae gaan tae Grampian Country Chickens either.

P.C. Don't worry. We won't put you to any of these people. Though we have had an enquiry from the Kemnay Knackery.

Parrot. Oo-cha!

P.C. But we've had a far more helpful call from a Mr McIntosh who is a bird fancier.

Parrot. Dirty aal man! Dirty aal man!

P.C. No, no. Mr McIntosh already has some pigeons.

Parrot. Foo's yer doos? Foo's yer doos?

P.C. Now Rover here does enjoy life. He looks forward to getting his drinking bowl filled.

Parrot. I like a dram. I like a dram.

P.C. What's your favourite whisky?

Parrot. I like a Grouse. I like a Grouse.

P.C. Most parrots don't fly, but Rover is . . .

Parrot. Fleein aa the time. Fleein aa the time.

P.C. Could we talk now about your sleeping habits?

Parrot. I'm a bachelor. I'm a bachelor. A peer aal bachie.

P.C. You've never been married?

Parrot. Seventy-two an never hid sex.

P.C. Seventy-two and never had sex?

Parrot. Nae for wint o tryin. Nae for wint o tryin.

P.C. So what was the problem?

Parrot. Miss Christie widna let me. Miss Christie widna let me. An I dinna like her. I dinna like Miss Christie.

P.C. All right, changing the subject, I'd like to talk about your diet, because back in the South American jungle your staple diet was insects.

Parrot. Horny golachs. Horny golachs.

P.C. But all that changed when you came to Auchterturra.

Parrot. Mince an tatties. Mince an tatties.

P.C. And how do you feel after eating a plate of Miss Christie's mince and tatties?

Parrot. Sick as a parrot! Sick as a parrot!

Horny golach: Particularly succulent South American earwig (for further details see *Teach Yourself entymology* as featured in 'Bruce and the Spider' *Scotland the What?* Vol 1, p. 36)

Foo's yer doos?: Characteristic greeting of N.E. man. No literal translation is known, but the expression indicates a courteous concern for the well-being of the addressee's joinery, plumbing and other working parts.

Sick as a parrot: It was in the role of Rover the parrot that Steve achieved the ultimate in the art of make-up – see photograph of him below taken during an actual performance.

Nicky Tams

Steve sings first verse of the well-known ballad straight through.

George. The divine sound which you have just heard is one of the great bothy ballads of the North-East. That of course is the North-East of Scotland, not the North-East of Great Britain which lies somewhere between Newcastle and Sunderland. To the true Scot this ballad conveys the whole ethos of his native land, but what does it mean to the more foreign or English ear? Perhaps we can begin again?

S.   H'aye.

G.   After 3

S.   Aye fairly.

G.   1, 2

G & S. 3:

S.   Fan I wis only twelve-year-aal I left the village skweel.

G.   The poet regrets that he did not enjoy the benefits of a comprehensive education.

S.   My faither fee'd me tae the mains tae earn my milk an meal.

G.   The poet's father launches him on a career in agriculture.

S.   First I pit on my narra briks tae hap my spinnle trams.

G.   For his working clothes the poet favours a pair of designer jeans.

S.   And buckled roon my knappin knees a pair o Nicky Tams.

G.   And in the interests of hygiene hitches them up round the lower part of his leg – thus – with a piece of suitable material, purchased no doubt from a leading fashion house, Yves St. Laurent or McKays of Queen Street.

S.   First I got on for bailie loon.

G.   The poet's first appointment is that of junior administrative assistant in the cow-shed.

S.   Then I got on for third.

G.   Thereafter he receives a preferment, being created executive officer in the pig sty.

S.   Then of course I hid tae get the horseman's grippin word.

G.   It would appear that the poet receives an urgent communication from Lester Piggott.

S.   A loaf o breid tae be my piece –

G.   The poet recalls his simple high fibre diet.

S.   – and a bottle for drinkin drams.

G.   – washed down by low alcohol Chivas Regal.

S.   Oh ye'll never get through the caff hoose door withoot yer Nicky Tams.

G.   The accessory is particularly essential when entering the bovine maternity suite.

S.   I'm coortin bonny Annie noo, Rab Tamson's kitchie deem.

G.   The poet becomes aware of his awakening sexuality.

S.   She is five and forty and I'm but seventeen.

G.   The poet sings of his Oedipus complex.

S.   She clarts a muckle piece tae me wi different kinds o jams.

G.   The relationship brings to his diet a welcome supplement of carbohydrate, glucose and vitamin C.

S.   'Cos I really turn her on fan I've got on my Nicky Tams.

G.   Evidence here of the garment's erotic properties.

S.   So – fan *we* get wed an ging tae wir bed
We winna tak aff wir claes.

I'll keep on my Nicky Tams
An she'll keep on her steys.

G.   The poet and his inamorata evolve an infallible method of
contraception.

S.   Aye, I hinna got a nicht-shirt, I've a pair o new jim-jams
An I canna get them aff if I keep on my Nicky Tams.

G & S. Oh – ye canna get yer pyjamas aff,
If ye're wearin Nicky Tams.

Newcastle and Sunderland: Two towns in N.E. England – the Rhynie and Clatt of Northumbria.

Oedipus: Complex character actor (Greek, 5th century B.C.) Began his career as a Jolson impersonator – his version of 'Mammy' won the Eurovision Song Contest for Thebes – but he developed into a precursor of Scotland the What? as a purveyor of Doric tragedy.

Bovine maternity suite: This is an erudite, i.e. unfunny, joke by the interpreter, who knows perfectly well that 'caff' means 'chaff' and has nothing to do with young cows.

The New MP

The scene is the House of Commons. An MP (Buff) is asleep on a green bench. The voice of Mr Speaker is heard.

Speaker. Honourable and Right Honourable Members of the House of Commons, pray silence for a maiden speech by the Honourable Member for Auchterturra, Mr Alexander Swick.

At the sound of his name, Swick wakes up with a start and gets up.

Swick. Sorry, sorry, Mr Speaker. But I wis haein a richt fine snooze. An I'm nae the only een. Look at aat boy stretched oot on the Government Front Bench. And he's the Minister for Energy. Eh? Wakeham? I'm nae gaan tae wake him. It's your job tae wake him. An ye'll hae a job. Look at that newspaper ower his face. It's the *News o the World*. He's been sleepin there since Sunday.

I know many Honourable Members will be wondering what my theme is today. I've jist heard Gerald Kaufman askin, 'Fit the hell's he spikkin' aboot?' Weel, I'll tell ye my theme, Mr Speaker, it is – Let us cut back on the cuts; Let us restrict the restrictions; Let us economise on the economies. 'Cos I mean, there's cuts aa wye. Take health – take medicine. An nae mony folk can at £3.40 a prescription. And what about the so-called NHS reforms. Last wik in Aiberdeen a boy came up tae me in the street wi a petition and said, 'Do you support a hospital trus'?' I says, 'Fit wye should I support a hospital trus'? The een I got's deen naething for me. Maist o the time I'm scared tae cough.'

Second, take cuts in the Armed Forces. They're spikkin aboot abolishin the Gordon Highlanders. I'm proud tae say I did twaa years' National Service in the Gordon Highlanders – an all I can say is – I wish tae God they'd been abolished afore I wis called up.

No – seriously, Mr Speaker. I still recall the esprit de corps of the barrack room, the friendly bark of the drill sergeant on the parade ground, the warm camaraderie of the ablutions fatigue, the expectant hush during the showing of the VD film and the nervous laughter efter it, and the anxious comparing of – notes.

The next cut I wish to attack has been proposed by the Right Honourable Member for Chesterfield, Mr Tony Benn on behalf of the Government. Fit's aat Mr Speaker? Tony Benn's on oor side? Weel, he spiks affa posh for a Labour boy. Ye couldna imagine Ron Brown spikkin like aat. Every sentence grammatical? Onywye, ye ken fit he wints tae dae? He wints tae abolish the monarchy, at a time fan there's three million on the dole already. If ye pit the Royal Family oot o work an aa, aat wid pit it up tae nearly four million. Weel, I'm nae for it. 'Cos it's my constituents

150

that are affected. I mean, Balmoral's in my constituency. I wis holdin a surgery in the John Brown function suite in the Glaikit Stirk fan fa should turn up but the Queen. I spotted her richt awaa tryin tae jump the queue. I had tae pit er tae the back o the queue. I said, 'Sorry my dear, tax payers first.' Onywye, twaa oors later she got her shottie and I says, 'Fit's the problem?' 'I'm feart for my job,' she says. 'An it's nae fair. Look at the struggle I've hid. Fower bairns tae bring up. Haein tae bide in a tied hoose. Nae jist one tied hoose. Half a dizzen tied hooses. Workin unsocial hours. I dinna ken onybody else that works every Christmas Day. And fa else has tae sit through the hale o the Royal Variety Performance?' Weel, I had tae agree wi her. And then she says, 'An what are my promotion prospects? Neen. I'm in a deed-end job.' So I says, 'Dinna you worry, Brother Queen, I'll pit in a wordie for ye.'

Aat's aboot it aa, Mr Speaker. I winna tak up nae mair o yer time. It hisna escaped my notice that Honourable and Right Honourable Members hiv started driftin awaa. In fact, I hinna seen the place sae empty since Scottish Question Time. I ken fit it is. It's openin time. Aabody's awaa tae the bar.

Speaker. Order, order.

Swick. Thanks very much. I'll hae a pint o export an a packet o cheese an onion crisps.

John Brown Function Suite: John Brown was Queen Victoria's ghillie, and his function has in fact been the subject of considerable debate among historians and considerable gossip among the locals on Deeside.

Dinosaurs

Of ne-o-lith-ic life a feat-ure Was a strange gi-gan-tic crea-ture called the din-o-saur. It's di-men-sions were pro-di-gious Ev-en el-e-phants looked like mid-ges Be-side the din-o-saur. But the din-o-saur's brain was min-i-scule They were the stup-i-dest pu-pils in the school and in a soc-ial sit-u-a-tion They sim-ply had no con-ver-sa-tion. Well, as I

last time

-er

The occasion for this song was a fierce spat in the public prints and on radio and television between two former Prime Ministers, Edward Heath and Margaret Thatcher.

Of neolithic life a feature
Was a strange gigantic creature
Called the dinosaur.
Its dimensions were prodigious,
Even elephants looked like midges
Beside the dinosaur.
But the dinosaur's brain was minuscule –
They were the stupidest pupils in the school,
And in a social situation
They simply had no conversation.

So all the other primitive fauna
In their friendly neighbourhood sauna
Ignored the dinosaur;
And nothing could be colder
Than the ice-age ice-cold shoulder
They gave the dinosaur.
The pterodactyl, that high flier,
Thought the dinosaurs were dire,
And knew he was not on a winner
If stuck beside one at a dinner.

Now the moral of this piece is
That every other stone-age species
Ignored the dinosaur;
So it's a logical extension –
No-one today should pay attention
To the dinosaurs.
For the dinosaurs still survive now,
There are two of them still alive now,
And the problem, people feel, with them
Is how on earth to deal with them.

Well, as I say, the answer's easy:
As they did in ten million BC,
Ignore the dinosaurs.
In the twentieth century AD,
There's a gentleman and a lady –
The modern dinosaurs.
So ignore them – just don't bother
As they bicker with one another;
No new life should we manufacture
For Ted Heath and Margaret Thatcher.

Auchterturra TV: Late Call

The Pope. (*Steve wearing the papal zucchetto and Celtic scarf. see Vol. 1. p. 142.*) When I got the call from Auchterturra TV tae come here the nicht, I say: 'Nae problem, I wis comin tae Scotland onywye. I hiv twaa wiks o a Barratt time-share at Aviemore.' They say: 'Dinna tell us you fell for the carriage clock and the canteen o cutlery?'

Yesterday I fly in from Rome, and I land at the Glasgow International Paddy's Market. I am greeted by my side-kick here, Tom the Archbishop. I know he is greeting me, because he is wearing his greeting face. Tom say, 'Holy Faither, I am Winning.' I say, 'There's nae need tae be sae smug aboot it. And from what I hear, I'm nae sure aabody wid agree wi ye.'

Then I ask Tom: 'What's big in Glesca iv noo?' He say: 'Well, we're hopin tae get a new Scottish National Gallery in Glesca instead o Edinburgh. Could you maybe help us, Holy Faither?' I say: 'Help ye tae get the Scottish Office tae favour Glesca instead o Edinburgh? I am only the Pope, I canna work miracles. I mean, look at the Scottish Office's contribution tae Hampden – only enough tae buy the corner flags – at one end.'

Then Tom say: 'What news from Rome?' I say, 'Big news. A helluva row aboot the Sistine Chapel. Ye ken the Michaelangelo paintings? The Vatican District Cooncil wints tae tak them doon.' 'God-almichty!' says Tom, 'Is Pat Lally on the Vatican Cooncil an aa?'

Efter that, I leave Glesca, and I travel here tae Auchterturra in the Vatican helicopter, known to the College of Cardinals as the Pontiff's chopper, which I do not use very much. Not as much as I would like.

The nearest helicopter pad tae Auchterturra is at Balmoral Castle and I pay the courtesy call. I ring the bell. The door opens, and there is a beautiful Royal lady in a blue bikini. Is Her Majesty the Queen Mum. 'Fit like, Ma'am?' I say. 'Nae bad, Jock,' she say, 'excuse the casual dress, but I'm fair plottin in here. Is an affa warm day tae be polishin my daughter's fleers.' Then I say, 'Fit's that puff o smoke comin oot o the upstairs windae?' 'Is all right,' she say, 'Is Princess Margaret's room.' 'Thank God,' I say, 'I thocht they'd elected a new Pope.' The Queen Mum say, 'I'm pleased tae see there's nae need for that. But fit's this I hear aboot you bein nae weel? Something the size o an orange lodged in yer intimmers?' 'Aat's richt. Fit an affront,' I say. 'Bad enough the Pope inside an Orange Lodge, but an orange lodge inside the Pope!'

The Pope: Unsporting cleric, but currently best known for being chairman of the Vatican Branch of the Celtic Supporter's Club.

Plastic Card

If you withdraw a sum of money from the bank,
You use a bit of plastic card
If you're phoning or you're filling up your tank,
You use a bit of plastic card.
By the time the coming century
Makes its long-awaited entry
Cash transactions will be absolutely barred.
Using money is so scuttery,
You will even buy a buttery
With your little bit of plastic card.

If you get some rotten income tax demands,
You'll use your little plastic card.
If you're out somewhere and have to – wash your hands,
You'll use your little plastic card.
When you want to spend a penny
And you find you haven't any
There's no problem if the toilet door is barred;
In the gents or in the ladies
Your admittance fee when paid is
By your little bit of plastic card.

You discover at the Kirk at collection time
You've rendered all your silver to Caesar;
But when you tell the elder that you haven't a dime,
'Never mind,' he says, 'the Lord takes Visa.'

To unlock the bedroom door of your hotel,
You'll use your bit of plastic card.
When you buy a flag to put in your lapel,
You'll use your bit of plastic card.
If you're up for tax evasion
And you lack Ken Dodd's persuasion
And the sentence of the court is two years hard,
There'll be a softer option
I'd commend for your adoption:
Pay a fine and use your plastic card.

There's nothing that in time you won't acquire
With your little bit of plastic card
Why squander any amorous desire
When you can use your little plastic card?
Cos ultimately, maybe,
People will produce a baby

By a means for which I don't have much regard,
Not by passionate exertion
But the dexterous insertion
Of a little bit of plastic card.

The Lord takes Visa: Was this elder a Christian? Though we hesitate to question his integrity, there is certainly no scriptural authority for this assertion.

Big Nose

John (Buff) is seated at a bar drinking a pint of beer. Enter Willie (Steve) who sits down beside him.

J.   (*Addressing an unseen Barman.*) Gin and Tonic please.

W.   (*After scrutinising Buff's face for several seconds.*) God! You've an affa big nose, min. Is your name Johnston?

J.   No.

W.   Weel, there's a boy I ken – Andy Johnston, and he's got a big nose, jist like aat. Are ye sure yer name's nae Johnston?

J.   No. It's not. I'll tell you though. My wife's maiden name was Johnston.

W.   There ye go, ye see. I kent there wis some connection wi Johnston. And has yer wife got a big nose an aa?

J.   Well, I've never noticed.

W.   Never noticed? Foo lang hiv ye been merried?

J.   Ten years.

W.   Ten years married, and ye dinna ken if yer wife's got a big nose? That's terrible that. Hiv ye got a photie o her?

J.   Yes, I have, as a matter of fact. (*Produces a photograph and hands it to Steve.*)

W.   Weel, we'll jist hae a look at it an see fit size o a nose she's got. No, she's jist got an ordinary kind o nose. There's a plook on't though. Oh, no, it's jist a mark on the photie. No, I wid say her nose is aboot her best feature.

J.   Do you think so?

W.   Nae doot aboot it. Mind you, the rest o her's nae that ill tae beat. Is that her ain teeth?

J.   Oh, yes.

W.   An fit aboot yersel? Is that your ain teeth?

J.   Yes, they are.

W.   Weel, aat's lovely teeth aat. Jist you tak care o that teeth. Hey, her een's real screwed up. Did she tak aff her specs for the photie?

J.   No. She doesn't wear glasses.

W.   Weel, I think she should.

J.   Well, she is a little astigmatic.

W.   Short o breath an aa, is she? Here, has she got a name?

J.   Dorothy.

W.   Dorothy. That's a bonny enough name. An fit aboot you? Fit's your name?

J.   John.

W.   John and Dorothy. Ten years married. An foo mony bairns hiv ye got?

J.   We've three children. Alistair's nine and the twins are five.

W. Weel, by God, Dorothy's kept her figure. Maist o't onywye. Her ankles are a bittie thick, but nae bad. Foo aal wid she be?

J. Well, she's – she's thirty-six.

W. Thirty-six! Weel she disnae look it. And fit aboot yersel?

J. I'm thirty-nine.

W. Is aat aa? So ye winna be haein ony mair femily?

J. No. Three's quite sufficient.

W. Oh, aye. So ye'll be sleepin in separate rooms noo, are ye?

J. No, no. We're in the same bedroom.

W. Very good. Single beds, though?

J. No. We're still in a double bed.

W. Good for you, boy. There's life in the aal dog yet.

J. Are you a regular in this pub?

W. That is a very personal question.

Plook: Skin blemish indigenous to Scotland.

At a bar: When first performed on stage this sketch was set on board a train, which started off with all manner of brilliant sound and lighting effects. But for the purpose of having a photograph taken for inclusion in this book it was easier to change the script than to change out of our dinner suits and find a train to sit in.

I'm thirty-nine: No matter how good Buff's make-up was, we suspect the audience's disbelief was never truly suspended at this point, and latterly Steve persuaded him, not without difficulty, to increase the age of the character to forty-one.

Taxi Driver

Buff is about to address the audience when he is interrupted by a taxi driver (Steve) waving a chitty.

T.D. Taxi! Taxi for Gordon. Taxi for Gordon.

B. What's all this about a taxi?

T.D. Taxi for Gordon. Look – Gordon, His Majesty's Theatre. This is His Majesty's Theatre, isn't it?

B. Yes, and you are interrupting an evening of culture and sophistication.

T.D. Culture and sophistication. I've just seen Ricky Simpson oot there. Fechtin his wye tae the bar.

B. Did he make it?

T.D. Couldna get near it for cooncillors.

B. What's Ricky Simpson doing at His Majesty's Theatre?

T.D. He's jist bocht it.

B. Ricky Simpson owns the theatre?

T.D. Weel, he owns aathing else in Aiberdeen. He jist needs the Jint Station and he's got the hale Monopoly board.

B. I suppose being a taxi driver you'll know a lot of well-known personalities, for example, some of the Grampian TV personalities?

T.D. Grampian TV personalities? Aat's a contradiction in terms, aat.

B. Oh, come on.

T.D. Go on an. Tell me some Grampian personalities.

B. Well there's . . .

T.D. There ye go. Naebody. Grampian TV hisna spent a penny on a personality since Calum Kennedy took them to court.

B. What happened?

T.D. He sued them. He wis daein a show in their brand new studio and he lost his kilt.

B. Good heavens.

T.D. Aye, it wis set on fire by a paraffin lamp.

B. Have you had Calum in the taxi?

T.D. Aye. He never pays. Jist tells me stories. He's good value, Calum. He tells ye a good story. He wis tellin me last wik Grampian are tryin tae get Bing Crosby for their Hogmanay Show.

B.   Bing Crosby's dead.

T.D. Grampian disna ken aat. Grampian disna ken naething. They tried to get Martin Luther King for *Reflections*.

B.   So who else have you had in your taxi.

T.D. You name them, squire. Cliff Richard.

B.   Cliff Richard?

T.D. Aye, Cliff. I didna charge him the full fare.

B.   Why not?

T.D. He's a pensioner. Telt me himsel. Gets his concessions.

B.   I'll tell you one programme Grampian do well. The Sheepdog Trials.

T.D. Nae wonder. It's only sheep that watches Grampian.

B.   Who presents that programme again? Robbie Shepherd!

T.D. Robbie. Aabody kens Robbie. It wis me that got Robbie that job. I says til im, 'Robbie, they're lookin for a shepherd.'

B.   But it's not just show business people you get in your taxi. I mean there are other occupations.

T.D. Aat's richt. I wis spikkin tae Frunkie Lefeever.

B.   The criminal lawyer?

T.D. Criminal lawyer? Tell me een that's nae. No, no, they're nae aa bad. I wis spikkin tae David Burnside. He wound up my Grannie's estate. Took a bit o deein – she wisna deid.

B.   How about Frank Lefevre? You mentioned him.

T.D. I winna hae a word said against Frunkie. The only time I wis ever in court, Frunkie got me aff a charge of breach o the peace. That took a bit of daein – I wis on the jury. Canna tell me naething aboot lawyers. I wis spikkin tae Jimmy Mackay.

B. Jimmy Mackay?

T.D. Lord Mackay. The heid bummer. The Lord Chancellor.

B. Of course, d'you remember? A year or so ago he was suspended.

T.D. I didna ken he played fitba.

B. No, no. Suspended by the Wee Frees.

T.D. Sounds painful aat.

B. What about politicians?

T.D. I ken aa the politicians. I wis spikkin tae Bob Hughes. He wis tellin me he's a freen o Nelson Mandela. It wis Bob Hughes that got a street in Aiberdeen caad efter Nelson Mandela.

B. Mandela Street?

T.D. No, Nelson Street. Canna tell me naething aboot politicians. I ken aa the politicians. I wis spikkin tae Neil Kinnock. He wis up for a meetin. I says til im, 'Faar div ye wint tae ging, Ginger?'

B. Didn't he mind being called 'Ginger'?

T.D. He preferred it tae Baldy. He hid Hattersley wi im, his deputy. He's affa spluttery, ken? He says, 'Take us to 66 St Swithin Street.' I says, 'Oh, faar's my hunky?'

B. But they're the opposition. Do you never get any Government people?

T.D. Yes. Last wik there wis a big meetin an I had Ian Lang, Kenneth Baker and Tarzan.

B. Michael Heseltine?

T.D. Weel the ither twaa caad him Tarzan. He wis gaan in for a haircut. And Baker wis gaan in for an ile change. I says til im, 'Fit's your job nooadays? You get a lot o sideway moves.'

B. He's the Home Secretary.

T.D. Aat's richt. Full marks. An he says, 'Yes,' he says, 'I've been in the Cabinet seven years now.' I says, 'Seven years,' I says, 'Somebody broke a mirror somewye.' Onywye awaa he gings leavin Ian Lang tae pey the fare.

B.   Hold on. Ian Lang, Secretary of State for Scotland travelling by taxi?

T.D.   He his til. He disna ken his wye aboot Scotland.

B.   I know what you mean. I understand Ian Lang has never heard of some of the Aberdeen councillors.

T.D.   Some o the Aiberdeen cooncillors hiv never heard o Ian Lang. They're still complainin aboot Willie Ross.

B.   This is all very well. But what's this about a taxi for Gordon?

T.D.   Gordon. His Majesty's Theatre to Grampian TV Studios to take part in the Art Sutter Show.

B.   What's the full name?

T.D.   Harry Gordon.

B.   Harry Gordon's dead.

T.D.   Grampian disna ken aat.

Ricky Simpson: Legendary Aberdeen entrepreneur, who shares with Rod Stewart not only the same initials but the same Spartan life-style. It should be noted that this name-dropping sketch varied from venue to venue and depended for its strength on the fame or notoriety of local characters. For example other occupants of this slot were Ivor Ludgrove (Fraserburgh) and Dowpy Dan (Thurso).

Calum Kennedy: Gaelic crooner.

Bing Crosby: American crooner; Hollywood's answer to Calum Kennedy.

Willie Ross: Secretary of State for Scotland in Harold Wilson's administrations. His early profession as a schoolmaster had bred in him an autocratic streak: he was a firm believer in corporal punishment and didn't suffer fools gladly, which accounted for his unpopularity, referred to here, with the members of Aberdeen Town Council.

Harry Gordon's deid: Yes, but if he'd been alive today, he'd be one hundred and three. Like Robert Burns and Mr Wallace's grandad (see Vol. 1, p. 148), what a wonderful old man he would be. A great star on any theatrical bill, Harry Gordon styled himself the Laird of Inversnecky. We three natural-born wines and spirits, and denizens of the lower end of the feudal system, can claim only to be the orra loons of Auchterturra.

You're Here

(Tune: 'I'm here'. Follies – Sondheim.)

No disrespect, folks,
But during the evening we've gauged
Who's all here.
Are we correct, folks?
Like us you're, let's say, middle-aged,
Pretty near.
Oh, some are youthful,
Just a few,
But let's be truthful,
Most of you
No longer observe days
Like birthdays
Every year.
But you've been around and you've lived some,
And you're here.

Brought up in war-time
You lived through dried egg and the blitz,
But you're here;
Sang – for a short time –
All Vera Lynn's greatest hits,
Now you're here.
Hitler defeated – happy day!
Then you were treated
To austerity,
Life trudged on flatly
When Attlee
Became premeer;
Came permissiveness, you weren't permitted!
But you're here.

You've lived through Freddie and Harry S Truman,
Peggy Ashcroft and Paddy Ashdown;
Tony Benn and Tony H-Hancock –
Which of them is the clown?
You danced to the Beatles,
Drank G&T and smoked Players,
But you're here.
Read all the details
Of all Christine Keeler's affairs,
And you're here.

168

Saw Orson Thing in
Citizen Kane,
Gene Kelly *Singin'*
In the Rain,
You all saw *Psycho*
Where I co-
Llapsed with fear.
To-night you'd have rather
Watched telly,
But you're here.

Marriage and children –
And Spock laid it all in your lap,
And you're here.
But kids are bewilderin' –
Could you bridge the generation gap?
Well, you're here.
Politicians came and went,
Some were vicious, some were bent,
Has it made a blind bit of difference to you? No fear.
You've lived through eleven years of Maggie,
And you're here.

Remember the weddings of Burton and Taylor,
Lord Longford, Lord Hume and Lord Reith;
The band leader and the fat sailor –
Both of them christened Ted Heath.

Too old for discos,
You missed out on reefers and pot,
But you're here.
You trudge round Tesco's, Gateway, Safeway – the lot,
But you're here.
Nothing to prove now – there's the rub,
You're in a groove now – join the club;
Middle age
Is a stage
For which let's raise a cheer – Hip, hip, hooray!
'Cos we're in the same boat as you are –
Three middle-aged, middle-brows who are
Your typical television viewer,
And we're here,
And you're here,
And, let's add, that we're glad – that you're here.

Vera Lynn: Singing ikon, symbol of Britain at war 1939-45. During the period of uncertainty immediately prior to the Gulf War, Ken Dodd (q.v., p. 59) remarked, 'There's definitely going to be a war: last night I walked past Vera Lynn's house and I could hear her gargling.'

Hitler: German heid bummer and all-time baddie.

The Christening

An old minister (Steve) holding a baby, stands beside a font. He addresses the congregation:

My dear friends, we are gathered together today in the sight of God and the presence of this congregation, to join together in holy matrim – eh? Fit's that? Oh, I'm terribly sorry. It's a bittie late for that isn't it? I'm losin the place here, but I've had a helluva wik – three funerals, two weddins, a Sunday School party and a haircut; nae tae mention gettin my new hearin aid the same day as the Bible Class acid hoose party. Spik aboot ecstasy. Heh, heh.

However, today is the day of the christening. And what a happy day this is for Auchterturra Kirk: the first time we've used the Gillespie Memorial Font since the 1982 Burns Supper fan it wis pressed into service for bilin the haggis. Oh, I never noticed afore – it must have burst, judgin fae the scum roon the rim, that's never been cleaned by the beadle, dozy aal brute.

The time afore that wis the christenin o the McArthur sextuplets, which were born efter Mrs McArthur – our dedicated but myopic Sunday School Superintendent, hid mixed up her pandrops an her fertility pills. Fit a christenin that wis. My airms were sair, my throat wis dry, my cassock wis soakin weet. Six o the little b – beauties. One efter the ither. I said tae Mrs McArthur, 'I thocht they'd never stop comin.' She said, 'YOU thought they'd never stop comin.' Whether or not they aa got the richt names I've nae idea, 'cos I'd lost my bittie o paper an my memory's nae fit it wis. By the hinner end I wis makkin up names as we went along.

So thank you, Lord God, that today we've jist got the one sprog tae cope wi. And this little fella here is the son of our good friends Timothy and Sarah Hartley-Cavendish, who unfortunately cannot be with us today, because they've gone away ski-ing. Well, there's been so little snow these past few years, you've got to take every chance you can get. Yes, Timothy and Sarah, who a couple of years ago came up tae Auchterturra fae near Canterbury in Kent, seduced by the blessed tranquility of bonny Aberdeenshire and the fact that they made a killin on their hoose doon there, Buttercup Cottage I believe it was called, from which they moved to their present delightful home at Bogs of Oxterguff, just at the backside o Clatt yonder.

I well remember when I first met Timothy and Sarah. It was a fine spring day aboot a year ago, fan the hail-steens were stottin aff the reef o the henhoose, when there was a knock at the door of the manse – 'cos the bell wisna workin. I went to

171

the door and there stood this delightful couple, very well put on – hackin jacket, Harris tweed plus fours, fore and aft hat, brown polished brogues. And that wis jist the lassie. Heh, heh. Very tasty too, I thought, observing that the rough tweed jacket somehow emphasised the shapeliness of her feminine contours.

'Whom do I have the pleasure of undressing – addressing?' I quizzed roguishly, kennin fine they were the inabootcomers fae England. 'We're the new white settlers,' she giggled huskily. 'At least, that's what the locals call us.' 'That's nae aa they caa ye.' I muttered sotto voce. 'However, come in! There's a roarin fire in the study, and the lady of the manse has just finished a batch of drop scones. What an appetite she has.' Heh, heh!

And then, 'How are things in Oxterguff?' I enquired solicitously. 'Everything all right?' nae carin twaa hoots really. 'Ooh, ya, wonderful,' enthused Sarah and launched intae a great lang story aboot goats an organic neeps, an biodegradeable environmentally friendly fertiliser. To which I responded, 'Ye mean dung. I hope ye wiped yer green wellies afore ye cam through the lobby.'

'And are you settling into village life?' I asked. 'Oh, ya,' said Sarah. 'We feel we're integrated completely into the community and now we're very keen to join your Church of Scotland, Vicar.' Vicar! Nae idea, some o that folk. And she said, 'We're already members of the Auchterturra Community Council.' 'Oh, yes,' I said, 'and who else is in that?' (nae even kennin there WIS sic a thing). And she says, 'Well, there's Simon, the helicopter pilot; Rodney, the advertising executive; Giles, the accountant with Price Waterhouse. But we're not all Sassenachs on the Community Council. There's also Hank, the Texan tool pusher with Conoco.' 'Oh, that's very representative of Auchterturra,' I said. 'A fine body of men – all no doubt doing good work for the benefit of our rural heritage and the preservation of the Doric.'

Then I said, 'Excuse me for asking, but why do you want to jine the Kirk o Jocks? You look like a richt pair o Piscies tae me. Ye've even come from Canterbury. Indeed, the Archbishop mentioned ye in his Christmas card that I got fae him at Easter and his Christmas message wis that you had got a quarter o a million quid for yer hoose doon there and as a result ye were the spik o Canterbury.' At which point Sarah said, 'We're not practising Piscies, we're more Anglican agnostics.' I said, 'Fitever ye are, ye're still nearer tae God then maist o my elders.'

But in the fullness of time Timothy and Sarah were back at the manse, and this time Sarah was great with child. 'Oops a daisy,' I said. 'No,' she said, 'they've told us it's going to be a boy.'

'Oh, well done both, especially you Tim,' I said tae this big gype standin gazin

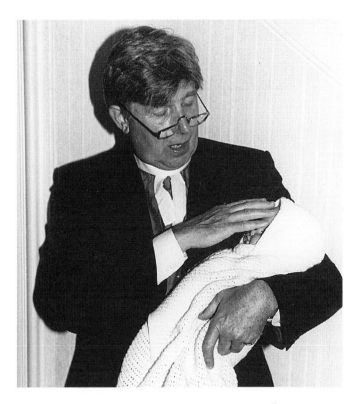

oot o the windae like a coo lookin ower a dyke. (I didna think he wis up til't, tae tell ye the truth.) 'Pretty good for a lang streak o misery that's never onything tae say for himsel.' And Sarah says, 'That's because in this family I'm the one who always takes the lead. Tim is the house-husband. 'Cos we're into complete role reversal.' 'Role reversal?' I says, wondering which was the bap and which the softie. 'Well, you will let Sister McKenzie at the Cottage Hospital know when you decide which of you is going in to have the baby.'

Well, my dear friends, as you know, in due course Sarah and Tim's union was blessed and their loins bore fruit in the shape of his nibs – our puky little friend here. So – in the name of the Father, the Son and the Holy Ghost, I baptise thee Rhuaraidh Hamish Angus Alistair Hartley-Cavendish. How's that for integration wi the community? What worries me is that Rhuaraidh is the name of the milkman; Hamish is the name of the plumber; Angus is the name of the butcher; and Alistair is the name of at least four members of the Huntly Football Club.

Clatt: Onomatopoeic Aberdeenshire hamlet, resonant of the sound of cow-dung hitting the floor of the byre. Note that Clatt has a backside; it also has a far side, but it does not have a front side or a near side.

Piscies: Adherents of a diminishing minor English sept.

173

Columbus

Voice / Piano

In Four-teen Hun-dred and Nine-ty two Col-um-bus sailed the oc-ean blue Fond-ly be-liev-ing that when he went, He would end up in the O-ri-ent But in-stead of reach-ing Hong-Kong or Bom-bay That clown went and found the U. S. of A. So we've a lot to blame that fif-teenth cent-u-ry chanc-er for Col-

um - bus Ba - by you've a lot to an - swer for

Chew - ing gum pop - corn

tales of Dav - y Crock - et Chris that's down to you . Mc -

8ve.

Don - ald's with a branch at Drum - na - droch - it Chris that's down to you.

Hate - ful Hol - ly - wood kids there's plen - ty ; Ram - bo one through to Ram - bo twen - ty

8ve.

Rock 'n' roll an' Co - ca - co - la 'n' Am - er - i - can foot - ball too.

last verse to Coda 1,2,3,5 &6

Chris-to-pher God-dam Col-um-bus All of this is down to you

1,2,3,5 &6 4.

you Chris-to-pher if your nav-i-ga-ter had made a left and

crossed the e-quat-or Missed A-mer-i-ca and sailed right round it

No-bod-y else might ev-er have found it But though you did-n't plan for it You

Dal Coda

sure got-ta car-ry the can for it. you Un-der the old star

spang-led ban-ner Comes the worst of A-mer-i-can-a Since A-mer-i-ca

176

In fourteen hundred and ninety-two
Columbus sailed the ocean blue,
Fondly believing before he went
He would end up in the Orient.
But instead of reaching Hong Kong or Bombay,
That clown went and found the US of A;
So we've a lot to blame that 15th century chancer for . . .
Columbus baby, you've a lot to answer for . . .

Chewing gum, popcorn, tales of Davy Crockett
Chris, that's down to you . . .
McDonald's with a branch at Drumnadrochit
Chris, that's down to you . . . .

Hateful Hollywood kids, there's plenty,
Rambo One through to Rambo Twenty,
Rock and Roll an Coca Cola 'n' American Football too,
Christopher Goddam Columbus,
All of this is down to you.

Heavy Metal, marijuana,
Chris, that's down to you . . .
Michael Jackson and Madonna,
Chris, that's down to you . . .
Folks from Birmingham to Buckie
Eating fried chicken from Kentucky,
Not to mention those jobs known as nose jobs,
Silicone implants too,
Christopher Goddam Columbus
All of this is down to you.

Open plan, split level houses,
Chris, that's down to you . . .
Big Payne Stewart's golfing trousers,
Chris, that's down to you . . .
Chris, you should be blushing crimson,
You're to blame for Mrs Simpson;
Wallis in the Palace, *Dynasty* and *Dallas,*
O J Simpson too,
Christopher Goddam Columbus,
All of this is down to you . . .

. . . Christopher, if your navigator
Had made a left and crossed the Equator,
Missed America and sailed right round it,
Nobody else might ever have found it.
But though you didn't plan for it . . .
You've sure got to carry the can for it . . .

. . . The Bacon and Lettuce and Tomato sandwich,
Chris, that's down to you . . .
The way they mutilate our language,
Chris, that's down to you . . .
Just to take two simple cases,
Chips means crisps and suspenders braces;
The pavement where I'd walk in New York's the sidewalk,
A lift is an elevator too,

Christopher Goddam Columbus,
All of this is down to you.

Happy hours with every second gin free,
Chris, that's down to you . . .
Donaghue and Oprah Winfrey,
Chris, that's down to you . . .
Thanks to you, Senor Columbus,
We've got Country & Western numbers,
Keep your heart in, Dolly Parton,
Which reminds me, *Twin Peaks* too,
Christopher Goddam Columbus,
All of this is down to you.

Oh, under the Old Star-Spangled Banner
Comes the worst of Americana,
Since America was created,
Whatever it does we imitate it,
What they do we do;
So if British women, God forbid,
Ever do what Mrs Bobbit did . . .
Christopher Goddam Columbus,
All of this is down to you.

Columbus: Temperamental Italian navigator who with funds provided by the King and Queen of Spain set off westwards across the Atlantic to go to India. The man was obviously a gype.

Mrs Bobbit: Oocha!

Mrs Simpson: Wallis Warfield Simpson, a principal participant in the royal soap opera of the 1930s, as was Queen Elizabeth, the Queen Mother, with whom Mrs Simpson was famously at odds. Consequently the Queen Mother's presence at the latter's funeral in 1986 caused considerable surprise at court. On noticing this, the Queen Mother is reported to have smiled sweetly, knocked back another gin, and said, 'Why should anyone be surprised? I've been looking forward to this for years.'

O J Simpson: A different Simpson, not the husband of Wallis, fortunately for her.

At the Palace

Mr Taylor (Buff) and Mr Wallace (Steve) are discovered wearing top hats and holding cases opened to display medals.

T. Weel, fit did she say to you?

W. Faa?

T. Faa? We've been in Buckingham Palace! The Queen!

W. The Queen . . . The Queen.

T. Fit did she say to you?

W. I'm nae gaan tae tell ye.

T. Awaa ye feel.

W. Weel, you tell me first.

T. Weel, I'd met her afore, of course.

W. Had ye?

T. Yes, oh yes. I was presented to her in 1964. When I was one of Aberdeen's typhoid victims.

W. Did she shak hands wi you?

T. Nae fear, would you?

W. Did she mind meetin you awaa back in 1964?

T. Of course. She asked me if my typhoid had cleared up.

W. She's very nice, is she?

T. Very nice, yes. We're very fortunate to have a constitutional monarchy with a human face.

W. I ken. Maks aa the difference. An I tell ye, she's much bonnier than she looks on TV. Did ye see her Christmas message – she wis affa soor lookin. She wisna affa cheery.

T. No. She was a lot cheerier on the typhoid ward. But I hid a rare claik wi her.

W. Hid ye?

T.   I wis telling her aa aboot ma job, 'cos she wis saying she didna meet mony jannies fae Aiberdeen. I says, 'I ken the feeling – you're the first Queen I've ever met.' (*Turns and waves in the direction of someone he has spotted in the distance.*) Cheerio – aye, aa the best – nice meeting you – cheers. Take care now. Cheers. Aa the best. See him?

W.   Aye.

T.   I think as a nation we over-rate our sporting heroes.

W.   Faa wis that?

T.   Sir Jocky Wilson. Come on then. I've telt ye fit she said to me, fit did she say to you?

W.   Weel, she says to me, 'I see you've got your award for services to child guidance.' And I says, 'Yes, Ma'am, I'm a lollipop man at Kittybrewster school.' And she says, 'Oh, Kittybrewster. I've just met your colleague Mr Taylor. He is the jannie there.' I says, 'Yes, Ma'am, and a very fine jannie he is too. Sometimes he's actually there when you're looking for him.' I says, 'I think he deserves a medal.'

T.   Fit did she say?

W.   I've just gien him a medal!

T.   I wis very worried when I saw you spikkin to the Queen – I mean, fit was the next thing she said?

W.   Then, she says, 'What an awful day of rain.' 'Yes, Ma'am,' I says, 'when we left Aiberdeen it was dingin doon hale water. Me and Mary is doon on a Golden Rail Wikend and we're going to *Les Miserables* tonight – if Mary feels up to it, 'cos her varicose veins is jist yarkin, yer Majesty.' And she says, 'Oh, that's not fine. One of my corgis had a bad leg last week and I had to have her put down.'

T.   Fit did you say to that?

W.   'Wish I could dae that wi Mary.' She says, 'I wish I could do that with some of my family.'

T.   Oh, oh – the young eens!

W. Nae jist the young eens. Her man.

T. Philip?

W. Oh, aye. She canna be deein wi him. Cursin an swearin aa the time.

T. Philip?

W. No. The Queen.

T. Is it true he likes a . . . ?

W. Oh aye. It's fit she wis tellin me. He never comes up the stairs tae his bed withoot a glass in his hand.

T. His whisky?

W. No, his false teeth – And then the Queen says, 'We only stayed together for the sake of the children – to make sure they don't ruin their own lives . . .' And then I got cairried awaa.

T. Cairried awaa by excitement?

W. Cairried awaa by two big flunkies – I wis gled to get oot in the corridor for a smoke. . . . And then I got lost in the corridor . . . went alang this corridor, got to a big door – went through this big door and ken fit I saw? . . . Charles and Camilla . . .

T. Charles and Camilla?

W. Charles and Camilla having their afternoon tea.

T. Having their afternoon tea? Fit did ye say?

W. I said, 'Oh, Your Highness, I'm affa sorry to interrupt you in the middle o yer tea an enjoyin yer fancy piece.'

Typhoid: The source of the outbreak of typhoid in Aberdeen in 1964 was quickly identified as a tin of corned beef sold at a local supermarket. The tracking down of the offending tin was a triumph for the then Medical Officer of Health for the city, Dr Ian McQueen, who subsequently was made a C.B.E. (Corned Beef Expert, as the grateful Aberdeen populace dubbed him.)
The authors wish to take this opportunity to refute the vile calumny circulating at the time that only in Aberdeen would more than 1000 people be infected by a single tin of corned beef.

Silver Lining

Buff sings to the tune of 'Spread a Little Happiness' throughout; George, apart from the second half of the intro, sings 'Silver Lining'.

Buff. Troubles seem to multiply,
They don't come one by one;
I've got quite a few just now,
Life is not much fun.

George. Well let's hear your troubles,
And if you can be concise,
Here is some encouraging advice . . .
And that's what friends are for.

Buff. Thirty years I did a job that I enjoyed,
Recession comes and I'm unemployed;
On the Dole at fifty-two . . .
What do I do?

George. Look for the Silver Lining,
Whenever clouds appear in the blue.

Buff. I can't keep up my mortgage payments – I'm depressed,
The Abbey National has repossessed;
On the streets at fifty-two . . .
What do I do?

George. Remember somewhere the sun is shining,
And so the right thing to do
Is make it shine on you.

Buff. I hinna got a job, a hoose,
I'm full of apprehension,
But I have got one thing that
I'm nae too ken tae mention –
A Maxwell Pension . . .
Now you find me absolutely destitute,
The kids are in care and the wife's walked oot,
On my own at fifty-two . . .
What do I do?

George. A heartful of joy and gladness
Will always banish sadness
And strife.

Buff. My story isnae finished,
In an hour's time
I'll be charged
With a serious crime . . .

George. So, always look for a silver lining
And you will find the sunny side of life.

Buff (who has reacted balefully to all George's optimism) shoots George and grins gleefully at the audience.

Maxwell pension: The many people relying on drawing such a pension were fated to be the victims of a very large bouncing Czech.

Dod 'n' Bunty

Dod (Buff) is discovered dialling. Sound of three rings – then receiver is picked up.

Voice. Hello.

Dod.   Is that Vancouver, Canada 561 5918?

Voice. Yes.

Dod.   Is that you, Bunty?

Voice. Aye, is that you, Dod?

Dod.   Aye, it's me. It's your darling husband, sending a message across the air waves.

Bunty. Oh, me! Fit's the metter? Fit ye phonin for? Is Auntie Maggie deid?

D.   There's naebody deid. I'm phonin 'cos I want tae ask ye something.

B.   Fit?

D.   Faar's the paper? Aat's the wye I'm phonin 'cos I canna find the wallpaper.

B.   Hiv ye nae papered aat lobby yet? Aat's three wiks I've been awaa an ye promised.

D.   Promised fit?

B.   Promised ye'd hae that lobby papered afore I got hame.

D.   I'll hae it deen, dinna worry, if ye jist tell me faar the paper is?

B.   Weel, it's in the glory hole.

D.   Oh, nae the glory hole. I can never find naething in the glory hole.

B.   Och, awaa. There's six rolls. Ye canna miss it. It's richt ahin the hoover.

D.   (*Grimacing.*) Oh.

B.   Ye hinna hoovered, hiv ye? Ken iss. The hoose'll be a tip.

D.   It's nae as bad as that, Bunty. It's worse.

B.   Oh, me. Foo ye gettin on? Feedin yersel aa richt? Fit did ye hae for yer tea the nicht?

D.   Soup.

B.   Soup for yer tea?

D.   Weel, I wis thinkin aboot daein mysel a suppie beef bourgignon wi sauté potatoes an mange touts, an then whippin up a passion fruit souffle. But soup wis easier.

B.   Fit kind o soup did ye mak yersel?

D.   Cuppa soup.

B.   Aw, Dod. I left ye twaa dizzen tins o Baxter's special Speyside Minestrone. Did ye nae see them?

D.   Aye, I saw them. But faar div ye keep the tin-opener, Bunty?

B.   Dod, ye're hopeless. Fit are ye? Hopeless. Ken iss? I'm feart tae ask – hiv ye been gettin on aa richt wi yer washin?

D.   Aye, nae problem. I've worked my wye through aa the shirts in my wardrobe.

B.   Dinna tell me I'm comin hame tae a basket full o dirty shirts.

D.   No, there's naething in the basket. I've taen aa the dirty shirts oot. I've started wearin them again.

B.   Oh, me. Fit aboot yer socks?

D.   Socks is nae problem. Naebody kens if yer socks is dirty. So there'll only be one pair o socks for ye tae wash. But foo ye gettin on yersel, Bunty, in Canada. Hiv ye got a click wi a Mountie yet?

B.   Oh, Canada's jist great. Aabody's sae nice. Ye ging intae a shop, or intae a bank –

D.   Bank? Ye hinna been takkin money oot, hiv ye?

B.   An we'd a lovely day for the weddin. An Fiona wis a lovely bride.

D.   Wis she? The wee darlin.

B.   I ken I'm only her auntie, but I wis greetin the hale time. I widna care, Maureen never shed a tear.

D.   I bet Maureen wis in her element bein the mither o the bride.

B.   I will say Maureen wis very considerate. At the reception she pit me aside somebody fae Aiberdeen, that I hidna seen for forty years.

D.   Oh, aye.

B.   You winna mind im, but his name's Arthur Ferguson.

D.   Arthur Ferguson? 236 Victoria Road? Twaa floors above the chip shop? Ginger hair? Monkey face? Looked like Mickey Rooney? Funcied himsel rotten? An ae Setterday nicht in 1959 he sneaked you awaa tae the duncin fan I wis aff ma work wi a blin lump?

B.   Div ye MIND Arthur Ferguson?

D.   No, I dinna mind Arthur Ferguson.

B.   Weel, he's deen affa weel oot here.

D.   Oh? Fit dis he dae?

B.   As a matter of fact he IS a Mountie. He's very senior. He's never married. He's never found the right person. He's married to his work. And he wis very nice tae me at the weddin.

D.   I'll bet.

B.   Aa the time I wis wi im, Art wis the perfect gentleman.

D.   Art? ART?

B.   Art's fit Arthur's caad oot here.

D. ART! There was a young Mountie called Art.
That turned intae a borin aal – dinna tempt me, Bunty.

B. Ken iss Dod? I think ye're jealous.

D. I am not.

B. Ye are sut.

D. I am not jealous. I never liked aat Arthur Ferguson. There's somethin nae richt aboot a bloke that can dae the slow foxtrot.

B. Noo, noo Dod. Ye're jist gettin ratty 'cos ye're missin me.

D. I am not missin ye.

B. Oh, weel, that's fine. 'Cos I've decided tae bide oot here anither three wiks. 'Cos Maureen's got a birthday comin up on the 29th o this month.

D. Fit?

B. Weel, it's a special birthday, this een. It's the big 5-0.

D. Big 5-0? Maureen's fifty-seven!

B. Weel, aat's her age in Aiberdeen, but aat's nae fit she tells folk oot here. Onywye, she's gaan tae hae a big pairty, an she's affa wintin me tae bide. She's invited Art as weel.

D. Art?

B. Yes, Art.

D. Weel, I'm warnin ye, Bunty. I'm nae threatenin ye, but if you bide oot there anither three wiks –

B. Aye?

D. By the time ye get hame, ye'll hae anither pair o socks tae wash.

Mange touts: Robust instruction from a health-conscious Aberdeen mother to her children, usually expressed in the original French, but sometimes in the local patois, e.g. 'Eat up aathing' or 'Dinna leave naething' or 'If ye dinna finish yer peas, ye winna get nae mair chips.'

Rave-up at Rhynie

There once was a gang of wild tearaways
Came roarin up through Fyvie O,
The leader's name was Dave – they were headin for a rave
In a park half a mile oot o Rhynie O.
They'd come across the moor at a hunner mile an oor
On their wye tae the rave-up at Rhynie O.

Now the leader o the gang – his hair wis dark an lang,
I widna say he looked like a monkey O,
But one fewer chromosome, an the trees wid be his home;
There wis hunners mair like him that nicht at Rhynie O.

Fit a racket, fit a din, an the locals aa jined in,
Jocky Bruce thocht Dave the leader wid be friendly O.
Said Jocky, 'Gie's yer crack.' Dave wis quick tae answer back,
'The crack I've got wid knock oot half o Rhynie O.'

Dod Strachan made folk sick, passin roon the cinnamon stick
That he'd kept in the hoose since the Forties O,
An twenty folk got high on a steak an mushroom pie;
Well, the mushrooms is magic oot at Rhynie O.

An orraman Jim Watt, he tried a suppie pot,
'N' ended up on the reef o the bothy O.
The stumer cam tae grief smokin reefers on the reef,
He fell aff an could've finished up in casualty O,
But his luck was in indeed, 'cos he landed on his heid
In the middle o a midden that wis sharny O.

At midnicht, jist aboot, supplies were runnin oot,
Ae biker saw the chemist's shop wis handy O;
He broke in an got a shock – there wis naething much in stock,
He came back wi a packety o Rennies O.

The Reverend John McGhee, he got high on LSD,
An his daughter, she wis soon the spik o Rhynie O:
For a puff o cannabis she wid sell a lad a kiss,
An for ecstasy, by God she'd gie ye ecstasy O.

190

Tae pit folk in the mood there wis drink an there wis food
An music fae a transistor radio;
The food wis really great – ev'ry raver got a plate
O hallucinogenic stovies O.

Wi that size mob, the toilets wis a prob.
They got them fae a famous son o Rhynie O.
Mind you I widna choose een o Farquhar's portaloos
At a rave-up if I hid tae spend a penny O.

Last year we went doon
Aa the wye tae London toon
Tae a rave wi the Rollin Stones at Wembley O;
Mick Jagger let it rip,
Well HE'D been on a trip,
Though nae as lang as oor trip fae Rhynie O.
But that rave-up doon there wis a Sunday School affair
Compared wi the rave-up at Rhynie O.

Cinnamon stick: Early (1940s) example of banned substance, a chewing gum and tobacco substitute combining the more repulsive elements of both. A corrupting influence on children who would smoke it while train-spotting.

Morning Coffee

Enter Stan (Steve). He stops at an imaginary front door and presses an imaginary bell. It rings. Enter Bert (Buff) from the opposite side. He opens the front door and looks accusingly at Stan.

B. Fit you deein here?

S. Are ye nae expectin me?

B. No, I'm nae expectin ye.

S. Weel, ye should be. This *is* the mornin ye asked me roon for my coffee.

B. Aye, but fan I phoned ye up tae ask ye –

S. Aye, last Tuesday.

B. You said if ye wis comin ye wid phone me back an let me ken.

S. No, no. I said if I *wisna* comin I wid phone ye back an let ye ken.

B. You said we should leave it that if ye didna phone me back an let me ken I wid ken ye wisna comin.

S. No, I said we should leave it that if I didna phone ye back and let ye ken you wid ken I *wis* comin. An I didna phone ye back and let ye ken. So I've come.

B. I can see ye've come. But ye're lucky ye've got me in.

S. I kent ye'd be in.

B. Fit wye?

S. Ye were bound tae be in if ye asked me roon for my coffee.

B. Nae fan ye hidna phoned me back tae let me ken. And then I did get a phone call this mornin. Aye, nae fae you, fae Bill Duncan askin me roon for coffee. You're nae the only een that gets asked roon for coffee.

S. Bill Duncan asked you roon for coffee?

B. Aye.

S. This mornin?

B. This mornin.

S. An fit did you say?

B. I said, 'I'll phone ye back an let ye ken.'

S. Fit did ye say ye'd phone him back and let him ken for?

B. 'Cos I wisna sure if you were comin. So I says tae Bill, 'I'll gie Stan a quarter o an oor. If he's here in the next quarter o an oor I'll phone ye back tae let ye ken that he's come tae me so I canna come tae you. But if he's nae here inside quarter o an oor, I'll just come tae you. So we'll jist leave it that if I dinna phone ye back and let ye ken in the next quarter o an oor, ye'll ken I'm comin tae you.'

S. Wid ye mind sayin that again please?

B. Aye, I says tae Bill, 'I'll gie Stan quarter o an oor. If he's here in the next quarter o an oor I'll phone ye back tae let ye ken that *he's* come tae *me* so I canna come tae you. But if he's nae here inside quarter o an oor, I'll just come tae you. So we'll jist leave it that if I dinna phone ye back and let ye ken in the next quarter o an oor, ye'll ken I'm comin tae you.'

S. Aat's the wye ye left it wi Bill?

B. Aat's the wye I left it.

S. Weel, aat wis a bloomin stupid wye tae leave it. Here, is this the last Friday o the month?

B. Aye.

S. Gee whiz! This is the day Bill Duncan wis comin tae *me* for his coffee.

B. Are ye sure?

S. Aye. It wis quite clear. The wye we left it wis if I didna phone im back an let im ken, he wid come roon tae me.

B. An ye didna phone im back an let im ken?

S. An I didna phone im back an let im ken. So that means he's waiting for me roon there (*Pointing to left.*).

B. But hud on. I didna phone im back and let im ken. So that means he's waitin for me roon there (*Pointing to right.*).

S. Weel ye'd better awaa roon there.

B. An you'd better awaa – roon THERE.

S. 'Cos one thing's clear. He's nae comin roon here.

B. Aat's richt. Hey, div you see faa I see, comin roon the corner?

S. It's Bill Duncan.

B. He's hopeless.

S. Ye spell the hale thing oot tae im. The wye it wis left couldna hiv been clearer.

B. An he turns up here.

S. Some folk can never get onything richt.

B. If he wis comin roon here –

Both. He should've phoned us back an let us ken.

Fit you daein here?: This sketch was usually performed, as printed here, in the Aberdeen street patois. When we were performing it in the Central Belt, Buff used a Kelvinside accent, Steve a Morningside accent – or was it the other way round? It didn't really matter, they both sounded the same anyway.

I've Seen the Day

I wis Mint-law's Jim-my Con-nors. Fit-ba' bas-ket ba' ath-let-ics tae Wil-son o' the Wiz-ard hid nae-thing on me I could

Last verse to Coda

rin some speed I could jump some hicht Oh I've seen the day but noo it's nicht. I

1.3.

2.

noo it's nicht We've an aal' tom-cat and he's past a' that Tho' he still finds birds ap-

Dal 𝄌 Coda

chase them on-y mair He can on-ly sit and stare at the birds Oh I ken the fee-lin'. Fan

Five in the dark an' five wi' the licht Oh I've seen the day

196

Spoken: *Aye, but nae the nicht!*

Fan I think o the man that I was in my prime,
Fit a lot o dirt folk spik aboot Time;
Time's the great healer – or supposed tae be,
Weel, Time's hid the opposite effect on me.
I wis Action Man fan I wis young,
But noo it's a different song that's sung,
My jints were eence swack, an my een were bricht,
Aye, I've seen the day, but noo it's nicht . . .

Fan I wis a loon I wis daft on sport,
I won a lot o cups an sic-like honours;
A terror on the tennis court,
I wis Mintlaw's Jimmy Connors.
Fitbaa, basketbaa, athletics tae,
Wilson o the *Wizard* hid naething on me:
I could rin some speed, I could jump some hicht,
Oh, I've seen the day, but noo it's nicht.

I mind fan I wis twenty-two,
A holiday I hid wi my brither Hughie;
On the Friday we walked the Larig Ghru,
On the Setterday we climbed Macdhui.
Nowadays I'm gassed, an my face gings puce,
If I walk the ten yards fae the garage tae the hoose;
Up the stairs on the bus, my chest feels ticht,
I've seen the day, but noo it's nicht.

We've an aal Tom Cat,
But he's past aa that,
Though he still finds birds appealin;
He canna chase them ony mair,
He can only sit an stare
At the birds – I ken the feelin.

Fan I wis young ye should've seen me drink
Whisky, vodka, gin or brandy;
On a Setterday nicht I wid quietly sink
Dirty great pints o draught nae handy.
But nooadays the bevvy's got me licked,
One half pint, an I'm up aa nicht.
It's affa fan yer waterworks arna quite richt,
I've seen the day, noo I'm up aa nicht.

In the early days of oor mairried life
We were baith in peak condition.
The *Kama Sutra* I gave tae my wife,
We sampled ev'ry known position.
It wis ten times a day and as a treat,
Twice durin *Coronation Street;*
Five in the dark and five wi the licht,
I've seen the day –

                but nae the nicht!

Kama Sutra: Definitive text-book of curries, tandooris and other oriental tit-bits sub-titled 'Do you fancy an Indian?'

The Operation

Norman (Buff) is in a hospital bed. We hear Alex's (Steve's) voice off-stage.

A. Oh ya! Oh, it's affa sair! Oh ya!

N. Fit are they deein til ye, Alex? Are ye aaricht?

A. Aye, I'm aaricht but this is murder! Oh ya!

N. God, I canna stand hearin folk that's in pain. Fit's happenin tae ye?

A. I canna get the elastoplast aff the hairy bit o my airm. Oh ya! Oh – that's it, that's it. Ken iss, Norman, that's twaa wiks I've been in this hospital and that wis the worst o't. But that's me ready now. Ready to get hame.

N. Oh, I wish I wis you. I wish I wis gettin oot.

A. Gettin oot – God, Norman, you jist got in.

N. I dinna like hospitals – they aye seem to be full o folk that's nae weel.

A. Noo, Norman – ye're in the best place.

N. Weel, that's fit aabody says but I'm still worried aboot it – I've never had an operation afore.

A. Norman – there's jist naethin to worry aboot. Hip replacement's jist a caker nooadays. God, there's a 99% success rate.

N. Weel, that's fit I'm worried aboot. I've never nae luck in raffles either.

A. Oh, now Norman, you couldna be in better hands. I bet they're makin a richt fuss o you are they?

N. Weel, I will say there was a boy cam in aboot jist now and he put a mark on my leg.

A. A mark on your leg, Norman. Weel, you see that's a big step forward that.

N. Aye, a mark wi a black felt pen.

A.   A black felt pen, Norman?

N.   Fit wye is it a black mark that he maks?

A.   It's a mark o respect, Norman. Jist in case. Mind you, mind you, Norman, the lad that got deen afore me, he'd a birth mark on his good leg.

N.   Weel I've a birth mark on *my* good leg.

A.   Weel, best o luck to you Norman. Here's hopin they get the richt leg wi you.

N.   Tell me this. Does the operation tak a lang time?

A.   Weel, it depends, Norman.

N.   Depends on fit?

A.   Depends if they're in a hurry to get hame for their tea. And on a Friday efterneen – weel, ye ken fit it's like yersel, Norman – it's the end o the wik – spik aboot slap-dash an through ither . . .

N.   Weel, I'm bein deen on a Friday.

A.   Aye, so I was hearin, Norman – Friday 13th. So faa's deein your operation?

N.   They tell me it's a Mr MacDonald.

A.   . . . Oh, ye'll be aaricht wi Mr MacDonald. He's a local man. His aal man's the butcher at Lumphanan.

N.   So, Mr MacDonald's jist cairryin on the family trade?

A.   Weel, that's aboot the size o't, Norman, aye. And then on a Friday efterneen they dinna need him in the shop, so he jist takes a turnie into toon on the bus and does twaa or three operations.

N.   Awaa ye go – that's nae richt – ye devil that ye are. There's nae a bus fae Lumphanan on a Friday!

A.   Aat's richt – I'm jist haein ye on, but certainly Friday is yer best day if ye're getting Mr MacDonald.

N.   Fit wye?

A. He's aye sober on a Friday.

N. Weel, the sister wis tellin me Mr MacDonald's an experienced surgeon.

A. Very experienced, Norman.

N. An she wis sayin he's studied a lot.

A. Studied a lot! God, he took fifteen years to get through the varsity!

N. Ahh.

A. Tell me Norman, have ye been spikkin to the ither lads in the ward here?

N. No, I dinna like spikkin to folk I dinna ken.

A. Weel, ye're nae exactly Terry Wogan wi folk ye div ken.

N. So fan I'm in among strangers, I jist ging richt into my buckie.

A. Buckie – God, it's mair like Siberia wi you, Norman.

N. So I've jist had my nose beeried in my book.

A. Oh, ye're readin a book are you, Norman? And fit are ye readin?

N. The life story of Douglas Bader.

A. Ah weel, Norman – there's aye somebody worse aff then yersel.

N. So I hinna been spikkin to nane o the lads on the ward. But you'll ken them aa, will you?

A. Ken them aa. Fine bunch o lads here. See that lad ower by the door there?

N. Aye, he disna look weel.

A. No, he's had a bad time this filie, that lad. Five years ago he was in to get a bypass.

N. A bypass? Five years ago? God, that's twaa year afore Inverurie got ane!

A. See that lad ower there – straight ower there wi the worried look on his face?

He hasnae been tae the bathroom for three days.

N.   God, I've only been in three oors and I've been five times already.

A.   See the young lad there wi the tranny, Norman?

N.   Oh, the young lad, aye.

A.   Weel, he's a young lad but he's an aal hand at the game. Last year he was in to get a vasectomy.

N.   A vasectomy? Weel, at least I'm past that.

A.   Oh, ye nivver ken – ye nivver ken. Look at Charlie Chaplin!

N.   Faar aboot? Ken, I used to like Charlie Chaplin. There wis een of his pictures an ye ken this, Alex, he very nearly made me laugh.

A.   Weel, weel by this time next wik, Norman, ye'll be laughin aa ower yer face because the hale thing'll be past and deen wi.

N.   Oh, I'm nae sae sure aboot that – I've heard aboot folk nae comin oot o the anaesthetic.

A.   The anaesthetic, Norman – God, nowadays ye hardly get an anaesthetic!

N.   I winna get an anaesthetic!

A.   No, ye jist get a jab on the back o yer hand, Norman. That's yer sedative, ye see.

N.   Fit's that?

A.   It maks ye feel dozy. Maks ye feel fine an dozy. Mind you, Norman – you maybe winna even need a sedative. No, no ye'll jist ging into a lovely dwam – a lovely dwam. An they turn you ower on your side and give you a lumbar puncture.

N.   Faa gies me that?

A.   Weel, it's your anaesthetist lad. Ye'll have met your anaesthetist?

N.   Aye, Dr Mushtaq Ahmed . . .

A. It's Dr Mushtaq Ahmed that'll gie ye yer local anaesthetic.

N. Oh, I dinna ken aboot that – Dr Mushtaq Ahmed's nae local. He's never even heard o Lumphanan.

A. Weel, of course he hisnae, Norman. God – he's fae the Far East.

N. Weel, he's never heard o Boddam either.

A. But I'll tell ye this – he's a fine lad. A fine lad – Dr Mushtaq Ahmed – ye winna feel a thing. Mind you, ye'll maybe hear plenty. Sawin an hammerin an chisellin.

N. Sawin an hammerin an chisellin . . .?

A. God, aye, it's like a joiner's shop through there!

N. Oh, I dinna fancy that!

A. Nothin wrang wi a joiner's shop, Norman. God, yer aal uncle John wis a joiner. Ye never cam tae nae harm in his shop?

N. I did – I cut my thoomb on a roosty aal hacksaw.

A. But hospitals is different, Norman – they've got electric saws. An Black an Decker power drills . . . hedge clippers . . . God, I think they've even got a JCB through there, Norman.

N. Through there. Through faar?

A. In the operatin theatre, along the corridor an roond the corner. They'll gie ye a hurl in a trolley.

N. I dinna fancy gaan on a trolley.

A. There's naethin wrang wi a trolley, Norman. As lang as they wipe aff the crumbs an the custard first.

N. Aye, they'd better dae that, 'cos Tibby's gien me new pyjamas for comin in here.

A. Pyjamas? No, no Norman – ye winna be wearin pyjamas.

N. Fit dae ye mean?

A. They'll gar ye tak aff yer pyjamas.

N. Weel, naebody warned me that was gaan to happen.

A. Oh, aye, Norman. They'll jist gie ye a goonie kin o thing, ye ken. A wee goonie kin o thing – and naethin on aneth.

N. Naethin on aneth? I've tae tak aff my semmit?

A. Aye.

N. An my lang johns?

A. An yer Fair Isle jumper an aa, Norman. They'll jist gie ye a wee thingy to cover your . . .

N. Cover my fit?

A. Oh, nae yer fit – cover yer embarrassment, Norman!

N. Oh, fit a terrible place this is. I wis a lot happier fan I wis sufferin. I mean, fit a worry the hale thing is.

A. Norman, there's jist naethin tae worry aboot. Twaa wiks fae now ye'll be oot, anither month efter that – God, ye'll be playing golf, min. Is that nae good now?

N. Weel, that is good – I couldna play golf afore.

Douglas Bader: War hero and role model for Aberdeen University Air Squadron, which produced a whole generation of legless aviators especially on Saturday nights.

Semmit, long johns and Fair Isle jumper: Complete set of N E Scotland underwear, probably sold to Norman as a job lot at Isaac Benzie's closing down sale c. 1960.

Fifteen years tae get through the Varsity: Mr MacDonald was clearly an abler student than many of our contemporaries in the Medical faculty.

Dr Mushtaq Ahmed: World-class Pakistan leg-break and googly bowler, who uses his anaesthetic skills to mesmerise and immobilise English batsmen.

Hogmanay in Auchterturra

(Grampian TV Hogmanay Show 1992. Broadcast across the Midnight Bells.)

SCENE 1: Auchterturra late on Hogmanay evening.

We see the Albert Hall from which are emerging sounds of Scottish revelry. We see inside the hall where folk are dancing to the sound of a fiddle orchestra. Outside again, we see Alec (Steve) cycling past the front door of the hall. We follow him to the cottage of his friend Norman (Buff), where he parks his bike and rings the front door bell. Norman comes to the door.

A.   Aye, aye, Norman. Are ye comin oot tae play?

N.   Jist a mintie, Alec. Tibby's taen tae her bed, an I've tae ging up the stairs wi her bottle.

A.   Aye, it's a caal nicht. It's a nicht for a bottle.

N.   Weel, it's a half bottle as a matter o fact. Tibby likes haein a Glenfiddich in her bed.

A.   Oh, she likes a Glenfiddich in her bed. Weel, onything wid be an improvement on you, Norman.

N.   Faar's the action the nicht, Alec?

A.   Weel, Norman, the hale o Auchterturra is jist buzzin.

They stop – at this point they are standing in the middle of a scene of darkness and empty isolation. A stray dog straggles past.

N.   God, aat's richt Alec. Look at aat. There's a licht on ower there. Oh, no. It's gone oot.

A.   Aye, that een's gone oot. But look there's anither een ower there. In fact, could there be twaa?

They start walking

N.   Aye, there's twaa.

A.   God! There hisna been a Hogmanay like this in Auchterturra since VE nicht.

N. Wis VE nicht on Hogmanay?

A. It wis in Auchterturra. 'Cos the news took a whilie tae get through.

N. So faar'll we ging, Alec?

A. Weel, I think we should just tickle in tae a puckly places an see fit een we like best. The world's wir oyster, Norman.

N. Ken iss, Alec? I've aye found on Hogmanay that the best pairty's aye somewye else. It's never far I am.

A. Weel, it's bound tae be somewye else. Ony pairty that disna hae you at it is aff tae a flyin start. But ye've got tae keep tryin, Norman. Keep smilin, an ye'll find the pot o gold at the end o the rainbow.

N. Rainbow? At half past eleven at nicht? Fit a lot o dirt ye spik sometimes, Alec.

SCENE 2: Outside the Hall.

We catch a glimpse of a noticeboard bearing the name of the hall.

A. Here we are. The Albert Hall.

N. I wis readin somewye that Frank Sinatra wis here nae sae lang ago.

A. No, no, Norman. That wis the *ither* Albert Hall.

N. Oh, there's anither een, is there?

They notice a queue of people at the entrance to the hall.

N. Fit's the queue for, Alec?

A. I think aabody's bein frisked for drink.

N. Quite right, too.

At the front of the queue the hall-keeper (Robbie Shepherd) is interrogating a local lad.

H-K. Noo, Andy. Hiv ye got a bottle on ye?

A.   No.

H-K. Weel, oot ye go. Ye should ken the rules by this time. Ye canna get in here withoot a bottle.

N.   Is there nae a concession for senior citizens?

A.   Na, na. Ye're only allowed in here if accompanied by a ten-year-old.

Alec produces a 10-year-old bottle of malt.

SCENE 3: Hall Balcony.

Alec and Norman proceed into the hall and upstairs to the balcony from which they observe a rousing Scottish Country Dance.

N.   It's a rare band, that.

A.   Aye, very good. And they've got Robin Galloway for their compere.

N.   Fit wye did the Committee bother gettin him?

A.   Weel, if ye tak Robin Galloway as compere, ye get the band a lot cheaper.

N.   I dinna see Robin Galloway.

A.   They must've backed oot an peyed the extra.

N.   Weel it wis fair worth it.

A.   Ye see Willie Smith fiddlin? Fit a technique! Look – it's aa in the wrist.

N.   Nae wonder. He saves his elbow for the Glaikit Stirk. Hey, there's Nancy Paterson duncin.

A.   Faar aboot? Oh aye.

N.   You eence hid a funcy for Nuncy.

A.   Aye. I've seen the day.

N.   I will say Nuncy's very licht on her feet.

A.   Her feet's the only licht thing aboot er nooadays.

SCENE 4: Hall Doorway.

We see Alec and Norman leaving the hall. As they leave they have their wrists stamped by way of pass-out tickets (Notice saying: 'Get your pass-out here'.) They leave the hall.

H-K. Hiv ye got yer pass-oots, lads?

A.   No.

H-K. Weel, if ye're comin back, ye've got tae get yer pass-oot. (*He stamps their wrists.*)

N.   Fit dis your stamp say, Alec?

A.   'Torphins Egg Gradin Station, June 1944, Grade 2.'

N.   It's a funny thing tae use as a pass-oot fae a dunce.

A.   Weel, but it disna metter fit it says as lang as aabody kens fit it means.

N.   I suppose aat wid be richt. Aye, as lang as aabody's graded the same, like.

SCENE 5: Village Crossroads.

Alec and Norman are now walking along the street towards the crossroads at which some lights can be seen flashing on and off.

N.   Is aat a Christmas tree in the middle o the road?

A.   Aat's terrible. A bobby flashin in the middle o the road.

N.   He should lock himsel up for that.

A.   An I'll tell ye something else. Aat's nae oor bobby. Aat's nae Louis Buchan. Aat's an inabootcomer.

They approach the bobby, P.C. Murdoch (George Duffus) who challenges them.

P.C. Halt! Who goes there? Friend or foe?

N. Fit's aat he's sayin, Alec?

A. He's askin if we're freen or foe.

N. Weel, I dinna ken. We've never met the man.

A. Say 'Freen'.

N. Freen. But nae a close freen.

P.C. Advance, friend and be recognised .

A. Fit wye wid ye recognise us? Ye dinna ken us.

N. Faa are you onywye? an fit ye daein standin in the middle o the road?

P.C. I'm a police officer, an I'm directin the traffic. But it's no you that's supposed tae ask the questions – it's me. Explain yersels. What are ye doin walkin the street at half past eleven at nicht on Hogmanay? That's extremely suspicious behaviour. I'm trained tae notice things like that. Ye're dealin wi a professional here, pal.

A. But hud on. Louis Buchan's oor constable. His been for years. Fit are you daein here?

P.C. I'm Louis's replacement. Louis's been posted. 'Cos last Hogmanay –

A. Oh, I ken. Louis wis drunk.

P.C. Drunk in charge o a village. An if there's one thing the Chief Constable winna pit up wi, it's a policeman that canna hud his drink. So Louis's been posted – tae Gardenstown.

N. Hogmanay in Gardenstown. Ye widna wish that on yer worst enemy. I widna wish that on Hitler or Snocherin Simpson the scaffie.

P.C. An I've been sent up fae Kirkcaldy tae get a grip on this place.

A. An faar did ye get this flashin lichts? I've never seen Louis wearin them.

P.C. Aye. Fae what I hear, Louis wis often lit up, but no by electricity. So this equipment's in perfect workin order. It's the same wi aathing else at the police station. Louis clearly couldna cope wi modern equipment. His pencil an notebook's in tip-top condition. I've never seen a pencil wi such a sharp pint. An there's absolutely naething in his notebook – except a mystery telephone number.

N. Fit number wid that be?

P.C. 999. Can ye tell me wha's number that micht be? 'Cos I mean tae get tae the bottom o this. I tried ringin the number, but it wis aye engaged.

N. Come on, Alec. You ken aabody in Auchterturra.

A. Weel, I ken aa the faces. An I ken aa the names. But I've an affa bad memory for numbers.

N. Weel, weel, but we'd better let ye get on.

A. Aye, we'd better nae hud ye back if you're directin the traffic. Ye could be in for a busy time. The school bus is due on Tuesday the wik efter next.

A dog approaches the bobby as they leave.

N. I widna bother, Rover. It's nae a Christmas tree.

They turn to walk on.

SCENE 6: Outside Farmhouse.

N. Faar are we gaan noo Alec?

A. We'll jist ging tae Sharny Dubs – I can hear the music noo – that'll be the dominie showin aff again.

SCENE 7: Sharny Dubs, Charlie Allan's Farmhouse.

We see a scene of jollity. The dominie (George Donald) is singing something amusing (naughty?). He is stopped by Charlie's wife.

W. Now, Leonard. I think you must have learned that from the boys in primary five.

D.   No, the girls in Primary 4.

W.   Now, we've had enough of Leonard and aa that Andrew Lloyd Webber singalong. Next for shaving. Come away, Evelyn. Evelyn's gaan to play the spoons.

Evelyn Glennie plays the spoons – applause.

W.   Evelyn went to the The Royal Academy of Music.

C.   How long were you there?

E.   Four years.

Charlie/Alec. Four years to learn to play the spoons!

SCENE 8: Outside Farmhouse.

A.   We'd better ging in – it's open hoose ye ken.

N.   Weel. I hinna been invited.

A.   Of course ye hinna been invited. It widna be an open hoose if ye hid tae be invited.

N.   I winda wint tae gate-crash.

A.   Norman, ye canna gate-crash an open hoose.

N.   I dinna like gaan far I'm nae welcome.

A.   God, dinna say that. Or ye'll never get oot o yer ain hoose.

N.   Files I'm nae welcome there either. Faa's aa in there onywye?

Alec looks in the window.

A.   Oh, there's a hale mixter-maxter o folk. There's Clatt folk, Rhynie folk – an bein Charlie Allan's hoose, there's lots of media folk.

N.   Media folk? Media? Faar aboot's Media? I've been tae Clatt, but I've never been tae Media.

Norman looks in the window.

Alec and Norman are still looking through the chink in the window when they are grabbed from behind by P.C. Murdoch.

P.C. Hello there, pal. Whit dae ye think ye're daein? Whit hiv we got here? A pair o peepin Tams. Are ye no aware that under the Auchterturra Bye-laws Section 14C ye're no allowed tae keek through folks windaes withoot a licence? Hiv ye got a licence?

A. Weel, I've my drivin licence an my wireless licence.

N. Hiv ye nae a TV licence, Alec?

A. No, I hinna. But the TV seems tae work fine on the wireless licence.

P.C. Whit aboot you, pal?

N. I've got a dog licence. But we hinna got a dog. So ye could say aat licence is gaan spare.

P.C. So that's a drivin licence, a wireless licence an a dog licence. Neen o them authorises ye tae look through folk's windaes withoot the permission o the householder. Ye never ken whit folk might be daein in there. They could be takkin their claes aff, an indulgin in lewd an libidinous practices of a provocative and sensual nature, which, if perpetrated in a public place would constitute an offence. Oot the road.

P.C. Murdoch pushes through between Norman and Alec and looks through the chink in the curtain himself.

SCENE 9: Village Street.

Alec and Norman are proceeding along the street.

A. Hiv ye ever played the speens yersel, Norman?

N. Eence. Never again. I gied my leg an affa wallop wi a silver soup speen. Ye ken, that we got in a weddin present fae Tibby's Auntie Jessie. Great muckle heavy thing.

A. Oh, aye. Jessie is a big woman.

N. No, no. The speen.

SCENE 10: Outside the Glaikit Stirk public house.

A. Weel, here we are at the Glaikit Stirk. Will we ging in?

N. Fit d'ye think?

A. Weel, here we are at twenty tae twelve on Hogmanay nicht standin richt ootside the pub.

Speed up on film as they vanish inside the pub.

SCENE 11: Inside the Glaikit Stirk.

Wide shot of roistering scene, centre stage held by the McCalmans.

N. Fat's aat lads makkin aa that noise?

A. Surely ye recognise them, Norman. Aat's the back four o Buckie Thistle. See the boy wi the beard? See fit he's daein wi his fit? Aat's fit he did tae the Huntly goalie last Setterday an he wis sent aff.

N. Michty me.

A. Aye. He got an early bath.

N. Weel, by the look o him, he's never hid a bath in his life.

Norman and Alec approach the bar and address the publican (Colin Campbell).

A. Foo's it gaan, Colin? Are ye busy the nicht?

C. No, it's been real quate. (*All visible and audible evidence is to the contrary.*) So far. Things'll pick up efter closin time.

A. Weel, here's tae 1993 fan it comes, Colin.

C. I hope it'll be better than 1992. Ye know, the recession just aboot crippled the licensed trade.

A. Oh, I can see that. (*He surveys the packed bar.*)

213

C.   Aye, this is my Happy Hour.

A.   For the nicht?

C.   No, for 1992. I jist hope I'm still in business to have one next Hogmanay.

SCENE 12: Inside the hall.

SCENE 13: Outside the Kirk

Alec and Norman have left the Glaikit Stirk and arrive at the outside of the kirk.

N.   Faar til next, Alec?

A.   Weel, here's the kirk. We'll ging in there. We hinna been there for a whilie. I dinna ken aboot you, but I hinna been there since Acky Duguid's funeral.

N.   Is Acky Duguid deid? Aat couldna be richt.

A.   Weel, they beeried im.

N.   I didna ken he'd been ill.

A.   He wisna ill. Naething serious onywye.

N.   Oh, aat's nae sae bad, then. Fit wid be on in the kirk the nicht?

A.   Weel, it tells ye fit's on, look.

They read the noticeboard which proclaims: 'Hogmanay Watch Night Service 11.45pm, 31st December. Rev Archibald Chalmers B.D. All Welcome.'

N.   Weel, you can please yersel, Alec, but I'm nae gaan in there on Hogmanay tae listen tae an aal mannie gettin on tae me aboot my sins. Faa wints tae hear aboot that on Hogmanay?

A.   I ken fit ye mean, Norman. Aat's the thing aboot aal Chalmers's sermons. Ye aye feel he's preachin at ye. Ye're quite richt, Norman: we'll gie the watch nicht service the go-by.

As they study the noticeboard they are grabbed from behind by P.C. Murdoch.

P.C. Hello there, pal. What have we got here? A pair o heathens loiterin wi intent. Ye've got a guilty look aboot ye. Ye were just aboot tae desecrate that sacred notice-board. I ken your kind. Anither twa meenits an it wid hiv been covered wi grafitti of a blasphemious and sacreligious nature, by God.

A. Grafitti?

P.C. Grafitti.

N. Fit's grafitti, Alec?

A. Weel it's Gaelic. He's fae Kirkcaldy.

P.C. What's yer defence? Explain yersels. Dinna tell me ye're here for the good o yer soul.

A. Aye, we are. Aat's the wye we ARE here. I couldna pit it better mysel.

N. Hud on, Alec.

A. Weesht! Oh, aye, we widna miss the watch-nicht service. Hogmanay widna be the same withoot an upliftin message fae Mr Chalmers.

P.C. Weel, ye'd better awa in, or ye'll miss the kick-aff. An mak sure ye pit something in the box for the Overseas Mission, so's aa these starvin Africans can learn what a merciful God they've got.

SCENE 14: Inside the Kirk.

P.C. Murdoch ushers Alec and Norman through the front door of the kirk. Looking through the top panels of the interior doors they can see and hear Rev Chalmers (Steve) holding forth.

Rev. Yes, my friends, I like to think that Jesus would have enjoyed an Auchterturra Hogmanay. After a day with saw and plane – because imagine, if you will, that he was an apprentice in Wattie Gibson's joiner's shop – after work he would have been off to the Glaikit Stirk for a few pints with the lads – James and John, and Doubting Thomas, who could never decide if he was gaan tae hae an export or a lager. Yes, Nazareth was a wee bit like Auchterturra. It had nae electricity either.

SCENE 15: Inside the Hall

Back at the hall. A dance comes to an end. Alec and Norman walk off the dance floor.

N. That was rare that. I enjoy a Dashing White Sergeant.

A. That wisna a Dashing White Sergeant, that wis a barn dance.

N. Fit's a barn dance, Alec?

A. It's een o that feel American things. Fit an influence America his. Aye nae jist on dancin. On aathing.

N. Faas fault's that?

SCENE 16: Inside the Farmhouse

The Dominie sings 'Columbus'.

SCENE 17: Outside the Hall

Norman emerges and is picking up the bike when PC Murdoch materialises.

P.C. Hello there, pal. Where d'ye think you're goin?

N. Neen o your business. Awaa an stop harassin folk. Ye're nae in Kirkcaldy noo. It's maybe a police state. Auchterturra's nae.

P.C. I've caught ye again. Your conduct here is contrary to the Road Traffic Act (Miscellaneous Provisions) Auchterturra of 1889 in that you are in possession of a vehicle, namely a bike, that's got nae lichts, nae brakes, twa defective tyres an a bell that disna work.

N. Fit wye div ye ken that?

P.C. 'Cos it's my bike.

N. So faar's Alec's bike?

P.C. I've hid it towed awa. It was causin an obstruction to innocent and, in many cases, paralytic pedestrians. And you're just about tae pinch my bike. I've caught ye in flagrante delictu –

N. Oh, nae mair o yer Kirkcaldy Gaelic.

P.C. Caught in the act o gettin yer leg-over.

SCENE 18: Inside the Farmhouse

It is now 11.56pm. Charlie Allan sings 'The Old Folk on the Wa'.

W. Oh, Charlie, thank you. Look at Wattie there. He aye greets fan he hears ye singin that.

C. Aye, he's a big softie?

W. Never, never, he's a music-lover. Michty! Fit's the time? It must be nearly midnight. Quick, put on the telly.

SCENE 19.A: Inside the Farmhouse
SCENE 19.B: Inside the Pub
SCENE 19.C: Inside the Hall

A guest switches on the TV. We see a Grampian Hogmanay show with Peter Morrison wishing everyone a happy New Year as midnight chimes. We cut from Sharny Dubs to the Glaikit Stirk to the Albert Hall seeing greetings being exchanged and 'A Guid New Year' being sung at all three venues.

SCENE 20: Inside the Hall

Finally we remain at the hall where we find Alec and Norman.

A. Weel, time for wir party piece, Norman. Faar's the dominie? We canna dae it withoot him.

N. He's nae here yet. He's maybe nae comin. An we winna hae tae dee't.

A. Oh spik o the divil.

D. Happy New Year, Alec. Norman. Are we all set?

N. I'm nae singin. I dinna ken my words.

A. Ach come on Norman. We'll mak a kirk or a mill o't.

R. Now settle down folks while Alec, Norman and the Dominie TAKE THE FLOOR!

Alec, Norman and the Dominie sing 'Here's Hopin'. (Tune: 'Fittie Folk')

VERSE 1

D. The midnight bells hiv rung – a New Year dawns in the North East.

A. And hope – it springs eternal in the Auchterturra breist.

N. Here's hopin that this year the world gets better, if it can.

A. Here's hopin Salman Rushdie gings his holidays to Iran.

VERSE 2

N. Here's hopin Mr Major his time tae quaff a pucklie jars.
There's only him an me that wears wir sark inside wir draars.

A. Here's hopin he gies Heseltine a job tae dae him proud.

D. Like Minister of Transport far U-turns are nae allowed.

CHORUS

All. Oh – cheery folk, beery folk, Gartly folk an Garioch folk.
Folk fae New Pitsligo, fae Newmachar and New Deer.
Cults folk, Culter folk, absolutely plootered folk.
Tae aa the folk in Scotland here's a very good New Year.

VERSE 3

A. Here's hopin that in fitba this year things start lookin up.
An Peterheid or Deveronvale knock Rangers oot o the Cup.

D. Here's hopin that the Prince of Wales keeps up his royal chin.

N. Faa else is stuck withoot a job till their mither packs it in?

VERSE 4

D. Here's hopin fan the Queen's on her Balmoral holiday,
That she and aa her faimily come doon Auchterturra way.

N. Here's hopin Princess Anne gets wed in Auchterturra kirk.

A. And then Prince Philip stands his hand ower at the Glaikit Stirk.

CHORUS

All. Oh – cheery folk, beery folk, Gartly folk and Garioch folk.
Folk fae New Pitsligo, fae Newmachar and New Deer.

Cults folk, Culter folk, absolutely plootered folk.
Tae aa the folk in Scotland here's a very good New Year.

VERSE 5

A.   Here's hopin there's an Auchterturra soap on Channel Fower.

D.   An tae play the part o the kitchie deem they fly Madonna ower.

N.   Here's hopin hotel bedrooms get a more exciting look,

A.   An instead of a Gideon bible, they provide Madonna's book.

VERSE 6

N.   Here's hopin that this year Dan Quayle improves a little bit.

D.   Here's hopin for the next few years the President keeps fit.

N.   Here's hopin David Mellor gies his hair a better comb.

A.   He may sign on for Chelsea –

D.   Well he scores away from home.

    or (depending on the result of the U.S. Presidential election.)

N.   Here's hopin that Bill Clinton can achieve Jack Kennedy's fame.

D.   He may be no Jack Kennedy, but his hobbies are the same.

N.   Here's hopin David Mellor gies his hair a better comb.

A.   He may sign on for Chelsea

D.   Well he scores away from home.

CHORUS

All.   Oh – cheery folk, beery folk, Gartly folk and Garioch folk.

Folk fae New Pitsligo, fae Newmachar and New Deer.
Cults folk, Culter folk, absolutely plootered folk,
Tae aa the folk in Scotland here's a very good New Year.

CHORUS (*reprise*)

Oh – cheery folk, beery folk, Gartly folk and Garioch folk.
Folk fae New Pitsligo, fae Newmachar and New Deer.
Cults folk, Culter folk, absolutely plootered folk,
The folk o Auchterturra wish ye aa a good New Year.

SCENE 21: Inside the Kirk.

In the kirk Rev Chalmers continues to drone on from the pulpit.

Rev.　And now – hark! I hear the Auchterturra Kirk clock striking midnight, which means it must be about quarter past twelve. So I wish you one and all a very Happy and Blessed New Year. And do feel free at this time to move about the kirk and offer your own greetings and felicitations one to another.

As the camera pans back, we see there are only two women (with hats) in the congregation at opposite sides of the kirk. They clearly have no wish to greet one another.

Rev.　Oh, well, please yourselves. I certainly propose to bring in the New Year in an appropriate fashion.

He takes a swig from a bottle.

SCENE 22: Inside the Glaikit Stirk.

At the Glaikit Stirk the McCalmans are finishing a number. Alec is immersed in the festivities when he hears a phone ring. It is on the wall just outside the door leading to the back door. He heads for the phone pulling the door behind him.

SCENE 23A: Lobby of the Glaikit Stirk: Alec (Steve).

SCENE 23B: A hotel room in Hong Kong: (Ex-Pat.) Eileen McCallum.

HOW ARE THINGS IN AUCHTERTURRA?
(Tune: 'How are Things in Glocamorra?')

Phone rings.

A.   Wonder faa't can be? (Ring ring)
             It winna be for me (Picks up phone)
             Hello — faa's there?
             This is Auchterturra 213.

E.   Hi, there! It's me . . .
             I'm in Hong Kong
             But nostalgia's strong.
             I'd like a crack
             With someone back
             Where I belong.

             How are things in Auchterturra?
             In the post office across the square
             Is there still the Thursday morning queue
             Of old folks who
             Draw their pensions there?

A.   Things his changed in Auchterturra
             Now there's rural deprivation here
             The post office that once you prized
             'S been rationalised –
             It was closed last year.

E.   Is the chemist always open
             Any hour of night or day?

A.   We hinna hid a chemist since last May,
             And baith my quines is in the family way.

E.   Is John Wilson still the doctor?

A.   Weel, we hinna got a doctor noo.
             The surgery's a craft shop rin
             By an Englishmin
             Wi a great big plum in his moo.

E.   And the bank? The trusty Clydesdale.

A.   It's gone!

E.   What? that's a sin!
        So what do people keep their money in?

A.   Weel, aabody his tae hae a biscuit tin.

E.   Things have changed in Auchterturra,
        But does the train still wind its way,
        Leaving Rhynie just on 9 o'clock
        And reaching Auch-
        Terturra by mid-day?

A.   There's nae trains tae Auchterturra –
        Dr Beeching fairly saw tae that.
        So ye really need a motor car
        Tae travel far,
        Because the buses have –
        Here's the laugh an aa
        Been taen aff an aa.

E.   And the hospital?

A.   Converted!
        Intae thirty time-share flats.
        It wis bull-dozed leavin just the vestibule
        On the day the Cooncil decided tae
        Close the school.

E.   Rural services are going.

A.   And the powers that be just dinna care.
        The phone is all that's left to go
        (*Sound of phone going dead*)

E.   Hello, hello?
        Auchterturra, are you there?

SCENE 24: Outside Sharny Dubs.

At Sharny Dubs a musical number is ending. We see exterior first – Norman and P.C. Murdoch at the door.

SCENE 25: Inside Sharny Dubs.

We hear the sound of the door bell.

W. Aat's oor first fit.

English Person. Oh, how exciting! It's wonderful being part of these primitive rituals. I do love these old Scottish customs. They're so . . . old, aren't they?

Farmer's wife opens the door.

W. (*Off*) A Happy New Year, constable.

E.P. A policeman for a first foot. Well, he should be tall, dark and handsome.

Enter P.C. Murdoch (having taken off hat) palpably none of these.

Enter Norman.

N. Naething oot o three. Failed on all counts.

P.C. A Happy New Year tae ye all. But that's by the by. Ye've aa tae come tae the Hall. I've just got the news on my walkie-talkie that the Regional Convener, Councillor Swick, is on his wye tae mak an important announcement.

C. But ye'll hae yer New Year, first, constable?

P.C. Thank you, no. Never on duty. Unless it's a single malt.

W. Good. You'll have a wee one.

P.C. No. I'll have a large one. (*Listens to walkie-talkie.*) Here I'm gettin the message that the Convener's getting close. The car's just come through the passport control at Kennethmont, an he's only twa or three miles awa doon the main road.

W.   Twaa or three miles? Michty, he'll be half an oor yet.

N.   A hale oor if he taks the short cut.

W.   So ye've plenty time tae dae yer pairty piece, like aabody else.

N.   Join the jollifications – dinna be sae miserable.

P.C.   Naethin doin, pal. No in my line o business. In Police Regulations 47 Sub section C – While on duty officers will refrain from singing, whistling, humming, yodelling, or tap, clog, Cossack, Morris, disco or dirty dancing.

W.   So have you always been a policeman?

P.C.   No. I've had a few jobs back in Dundee. I had a job on board Captain Scott's ship, the *Discovery*. I guided the tourists and took the money. Then I'd a job on the Tay Road Bridge. I advised the motorists – tae cross by the railway bridge – the first one – and I took the money. Then I became a Dundee District Cooncillor. And I just took the money.

W.   Come on, this is Auchterturra. Tonight is Hogmanay. You're in a duty free area. You must be able to do something . . . recite, sing. We're not going to let you off.

N.   Aat's richt. We are the masters now.

P.C.   I only ken one song. It's a bothy ballad called 'Nicky Tams'.

W.   My favourite!

P.C.   Murdoch sings 'Nicky Tams'.

After first verse English person interrupts.

E.P.   Is that Gaelic?

P.C.   No darlin. If it wis Gaelic I'd be gettin a grant for it.

E.P.   Well what on earth was that!

P.C.   That was English. Whaur dae you come fae?

E.P.   I couldn't make out a word. We find it very difficult to understand what people are saying in Scotland. We can't even understand Eddie Mair and Jackie Bird.

D.   Don't worry, I'll tell you what it means as we go along. Just imagine the constable here is a young poet singing of his life and roots in a primitive agricultural community. Shall we begin again?

P.C. Murdoch and the Dominie sing Nicky Tams (see p. 147)

P.C.   Murdoch addresses the company.

P.C.   Right you lot – awa tae the Hall for the Regional Convenor's announcement. I'll awa tae the Glaikit Stirk tae round up the minister an the rest o the village.

SCENE 26: Outside the Hall.

The Regional Convenor, Councillor Alexander Swick, emerges from his car. The crowd presses in on him.

C.S.   Aa richt, aa richt. Let the dog see the rabbit. (*He enters the hall.*)

SCENE 27: Inside the Hall doorway.

As Councillor Swick enters the hall he spots a man being frisked by an attractive female assistant hall-keeper.

H-K.   Straight through Mr Convenor. Never mind the bouncer.

C.S.   Fit wye div I nae get a bosie?

P.C.   'Cos aabody kens that accordin tae Auchterturra by-law 55 nae cooncillor is ever allowed tae traivel withoot his hip flask. Through ye go.

C.S.   Aa richt Taggart. There's nae need tae gie awaa aa wir secrets.

SCENE 28: Inside the Hall.

Swick carries on into the hall and strides on to the platform. He is played on by the fiddlers playing 'I'm the Saftest of the Faimly'. He addresses the throng.

C.S. Ladies and gentlemen, tonight is a great day for Auchterturra. The sands of time his rin oot for the Aal Year. It has came to the end of its journey. It has had its shottie; it has shot its bolt. Now we stand at the cross-roads, waiting on the thresh-hold of a New Year for which ten short minutes ago the starting pistol gave the green light for.

My friends, I have come here tonight straight from a working high tea wi twaa or three big guns fae the Scottish Office, and after a full and frank exchange of views we reached a consensus that the sausage an egg wis fine but the scones wis a bittie stale. I always felt personally mysel we should hiv kept the Cooncil caterin in hoose – we should never hiv privatised the fruit loaf.

Here am I, the Regional Convener, takkin the time, trouble, an twelve quid attendance money tae come oot here tae the middle o naewye – in fact, it's nae the middle, it's much further oot than that – an in fact, that's fit I'm here aboot. It's come oot in the Brussels computer that Auchterturra is the maist isolated, remote an backward community in the hale o Europe and that includes Glesca! It could be in the world, but the computer's nae big enough.

Eh? fit's aat, Sir? I ken you ken that. We aa ken that. But they didna ken that till the computer telt them. Listen now, listen. This is the good bit. Because o that, Auchterturra's been granted a special Remote Area Subsidy. Ye ken fit 'set aside' means? Aat's richt, it means Charlie Allan o Sharny Dubs is bein peyed a fortune for growin a field o jobby nettles. Weel, under this special subsidy the hale o Auchterturra's been set aside. (*Reaction*) That means aabody in the village gets peyed a heap o dosh for daein naething. (*Cheers*) Aa the public services is bein restored, an the school winna hae tae close. (*Cheers*)

We see the Dominie's joyful reaction in the crowd.

It will be fully staffed and serviced, aye an nae by the kind o inspector that visited it last month. This inspector boy gings intae a classroom an says tae a wee loon in the front 'Give me a number between 10 and 100.' An the loon says '28'. An the inspector writes up on the blackboard 82. Looks for some reaction. Nae reaction. So he says tae the girlie at the front, 'You give me a number.' She says, '73'. And he writes up 37. Still no reaction. So he says tae a loon at the back o the class, 'You give me a number.' An he says '55. See if ye can mak an erse o that een.'

Ladies and gentlemen, that wee boy is a bittie like Auchterturra itsel. Nae much til 'im. Naething tae look at. But nae tae be mucked aboot. A Happy New Year to you all.

Full cast sing 'Auchterturra' (Tune: Oklahoma!).

Buff: It's hard tae believe it's anither New Year.
George Donald: It's hard tae believe we're in '93
George Duffus: But lookin aheid, if there's ae thing clear –
Steve: Auchterturra is the place tae be.
Colin: It's the place tae be in 1993.

Buff: Oor village Auchterturra.
George Donald: Although it is expandin.
George Duffus: It's hardly Edinburgh.
Steve: It's littler than Lumphanan.

Five Principals:
Never nae hassle an never nae sweat,
Never nae payment o the poll tax yet,
Never nae streets wi double yeller lines,
Never nae wardens an never nae fines.

CHORUS

Auchterturra! far the folk are couthie but content.
Een or twaa sick coos is front page news
And a funeral is a big event.
Auchterturra! but excitement often can explode.

Steve:
On a moonlicht nicht, ye micht – jist micht
See a futret rinnin ower the road.

CHORUS

The place we belong til is smaa
An naething much happens at aa,
But we're nae sad – No!
We're daein awaa nae bad – we're nae complainin,
We're daein fine, Auchterturra,
Auchterturra, nae bad!

CHORUS

The place we belong til is smaa
An naething much happens at aa,
But we're nae sad – No!
We're daein awaa nae bad – we're nae complainin,
We're daein fine, Auchterturra,
Auchterturra, nae bad!

CHORUS

We're daein fine Auchterturra,
Auchterturra –
O-U-can tell we canna spell
AUCHTERTURRA!

SCENE 29: Inside the Hall.

A.   Will ye hae a dram, constable? Nae hard feelins.

N.   Nae hard feelins.

P.C.   Are you tryin tae bribe a police officer? I should be rinnin the pair of ye in an lockin ye up. But I winna.

A: Is aat 'cos it's wir first offence?

P.C.   No.

N   Is it 'cos ye're full o the festive spirit?

P.C.   No. It's 'cos my wife's got the cells full o lodgers.

SCENE 30: Outside the Hall.

Alec and Norman witness someone being carried into a house.

A.   That's Louis Buchan been brocht hame. Michty, he spent Hogmanay in Gardenstown and he's *still* bleezin!

N.   It maks ye really proud o Auchterturra, that kind o thing.

Credits roll.

One character who has made an appearance in nearly every Scotland the What? show is local politician, Councillor Alexander Swick. But it's not generally known that the councillor has been present in the audience on nearly all our major landmark occasions, culminating in our Final Fling in 1995 . . .

1969 – Councillor and Mrs. Swick at home.

"Listen tae this, Sandy." Councillor and Mrs. Swick are invited to a preview of a new show entitled 'Scotland the What?' in the Arts Centre, King Street, prior to its opening on the Edinburgh Festival Fringe." I funcy that, div you?

No, I'm nae ga'n' there. Bunch o' overgrown schoolboys that should ken better. I suppose it's the satire boom reachin' Aiberdeen years efter a'wye else. I dinna like satire – it's nae funny. It certainly winna work in Aiberdeen. There's naebody in Aiberdeen worth satirisin'. Wait a minute, though. Fit dis that say at the bottom? "Wine will be served." So there's a gless o' wine, eh? Ach, weel, I think we should be seen tae be supportin' oor local artistes.

1971 – Swick and a fellow-councillor outside His Majesty's Theatre

Fit's this? Scotland the What? at His Majesty's? I thocht you said you wis takkin' me tae an avant-garde continental picter.

I'm sorry, Sandy. It wis certainly "Swedish Sex Capers" that wis on at the beginnin' o' the wik.

SCOTLAND THE WHAT?

1982 — Swick at the Royal re-opening of His Majesty's after the £3½M refurbishment.

I'm sorry my wife couldn't be here this evening.

Dinna worry. I'm in the same boat. This is Mary's bingo nicht. Hiv ye seen "Scotland the What?" afore? I've seen them dizzens o' times ower the years — theatre shows, civic receptions, cabarets — an' I can safely say I've never peyed for my ticket once.

1995 — Swick and Mrs. Swick at Scotland the What?'s Final Fling.

Well, well. Scotland the What? — Final Fling. Their farewell show. See? They're packin' it in. I telt ye in 1969 they wid never lest.

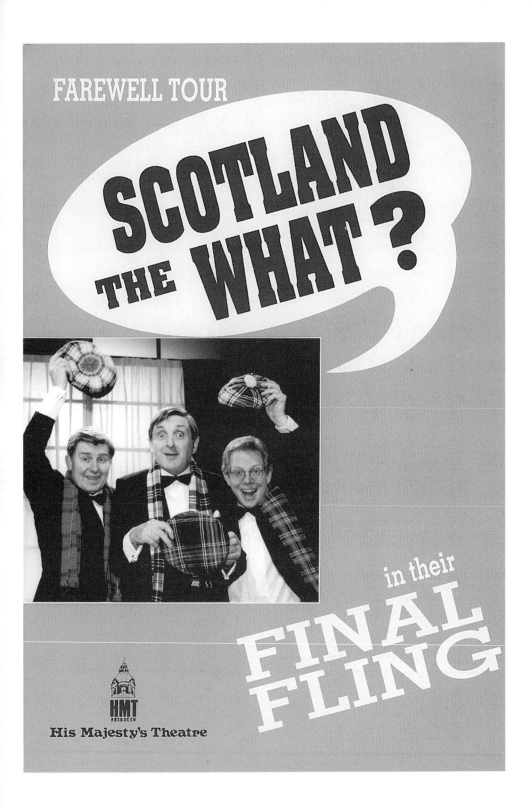

The Holiday Maker

The scene is the reception area of the Glaikit Stirk, Auchterturra's only public house. A radio announcement is heard: 'Here is a news flash. The Prime Minister and Mrs Major have left for a short holiday in Scotland. Their exact destination is unknown, but it is believed they are heading for deepest Aberdeenshire.' Enter John Major (Steve) equipped for a holiday.

J.M. The Glaikit Stirk. Funny name. (*Reads.*) Please ring for service. (*He rings; sound of a cow.*) Funny noise.

Enter the Landlord (Buff).

L. Aye, aye. Fit like?

J.M. I'm sorry?

L. Aye, aye. Fit like?

J.M. One moment while I consult my local phrase book. (*Consults phrase book.*) Here it is – 'Doric for Beginners, Sassenachs and the Intellectually Challenged.' Oh. Scored 3 out of 3. Now, what did you say?

L. Aye, aye, Fit like?

J.M. 'Aye, aye. Fit like?' (*Consults phrase book again.*) Ah, here we are: 'Nae bad iv aa. Aye tchavin on min.'

L. God, if it's nae Robbie Shepherd!

J.M. No. Just a happy chappy on his holidays. Looking for a bed for the night.

L. Weel, ye're in luck. 'Cos we hiv got the one bedroom.

J.M. You've got the one bedroom vacant?

L. We've got the one bedroom full-stop. Weel, weel, but we'd better get ye booked in. Are ye jist yersel?

J.M. No. I have a lady with me.

L. Aye, aye. We ken your kind. Dinna worry. Mum's the word.

J.M. No, no. It's my wife.

L.   Yer wife. Aye, aye, an I'm the Prime Minister. Noo how wid ye like tae pay for this?

J.M.   Oh, credit card or cheque.

L.   No. I prefer the local currency.

J.M.   The local currency?

L.   Aye, the local currency. Neeps an tatties.

J.M.   Neeps and tatties? Are these coins or notes? And if so, how many neeps to the Deutchmark? And how many tatties to the Franc? How do they stand against the Pfennig? Are they contained in the usual basket of European currencies?

L.   Oh, ye never pit neeps an tatties in a basket. For neeps an tatties fit ye need is secks.

J.M.   Sex?

L.   Aye, secks. Secks o tatties. Ye've heard o secks, hivn't ye?

J.M.   That's all I ever do hear about these days. But do you get sex in Auchterturra?

L. Oh, there's nae shortage o secks in Auchterturra.

J.M. Where do you get sex in Auchterturra?

L. Weel, ye get secks onywye in Auchterturra. Fan my wife's wintin secks she gings tae Jocky Bain the orra man, him that looks efter the pigs –

J.M. This is getting back to basics.

L. – an he gies her secks.

J.M. And don't you mind?

L. Weel, it saves me the bother (*He looks closely at Mr Major.*). Ken iss? I think I've seen you afore somewye?

J.M. Have you really?

L. Did you ever play skip for Alford in the Donside Bowlin League?

J.M. No.

L. Ye never drove the hearse for Sammy Bruce the joiner, did ye?

J.M. No.

L. Wait a minute. Television!

J.M. Getting warm. I have been on the telly once or twice.

L. *Coronation Street*? Ye're Ken Barlow wi glesses on.

J.M. As a matter of fact I'm a politician.

L. A politician? Ye're nae Tony Blair, are ye?

J.M. I'm not pretty enough to be Tony Blair.

L. Ye're nae John Prescott?

J.M. I'm not pretty enough to be John Prescott.

L. Ye're certainly nae Margaret Beckett.

J.M. I'm too pretty to be Margaret Beckett.

L.   Weel, ye've got me beat. I'll tell you, gie me a clue.

J.M. Oh, I rather like this. Good game, good game.

L.   Bruce Forsyth?

J.M. I'm a great supporter of Maastricht.

L.   I'm pleased tae hear it. My grannie bides in the Lang Stracht.

J.M. I'll give you a proper clue. I'd like to be good enough to play cricket for England.

L.   Sae wid aa the lads in the team. Nuh. I canna get ye. Yer clues is rubbish.

J.M. I know. I'm not very good at this kind of thing. Doing my best but pretty hopeless. I simply don't have a clue to give you.

L.   Wait a minute. Hopeless, nae very good, hinna got a clue? God almichty, ye're John Major!

J.M. That's right, I am. Just think. You'll be able to say the Prime Minister slept here.

L.   You hinna tried the bed yet. But excuse me for askin this, Prime Minister: Auchterturra's nae a famous place. It's nae a household word like Ryhnie or Clatt. Of aa the grand fowk that you ken, faa telt ye aboot a wee hidey-hole like iss?

J.M. Salman Rushdie. Auchterturra was warmly recommended to me by Salman Rushdie.

L.   Salman Rushdie! Fit a rare lad. Salman bade here for nearly twaa years. Oh, Salman fitted in fine intae Auchterturra. He became an elder o the kirk, jined the local fire brigade – he'd a great time here. He jist hid the one bad nicht – it wis here in the pub. Salman wis here, sittin ower there haein a drink wi Lord Lucan, an faa should come in but the local heid-maister – the dominie we caa im.

J.M. I did hear about that, yes.

L.   An I says tae Salman, 'Salman,' I says, 'This is the Auchterturra dominie.'

J.M. And he thought you said, 'the Ayatollah Khomeini.'

You're the Top

(A hymn to Scottish excellence. Music: Cole Porter)

You're the top, you're Ben Macdhui,
You're the top, you're a large Drambuie,
You're the golfing style
Of Sandy Lyle
At Troon,
You're the melancholy
Rev'rend I. M. Jolly,
You're Daphne Broon.
You're the Spey, you're Glesca patter,
You're a day – gaan doon the watter,
I'm the World Cup Team, Andy Roxburgh's dream gone pop;
But baby, if I'm the bottom, you're the top.

You're the top, you're Skye, you're Arran,
You're the top, you're Bill McLaren,
You're the kind of fee a Scots Q.C. can earn.
You're the Glasgow polis, you're William Wallace,
You're Bannockburn.
You're the top, you're a Tartan Special,
You're the top, you're Edinburgh Cestle;
I'm a whisky glass that's down to its last wee drop,
But, baby, if I'm the bottom you're the top.

You're the top, you're the late great Andy,
You're the top, you're Para Handy,
You're McGonagill singing of the sil-v'ry Tay,
You're a snooker cench'ry by Stephen Hendry,
You're Hogmanay.
You're the top, you're a fine long blether,
You're the top, you're McCaskill's weather;
I'm Ian Lang gettin maist things wrang – a flop!
But baby, if I'm the bottom, you're the top.

Ian Lang gettin maist things wrang: by its nature, this song tends to be full of references which inevitably date: Ian Lang was Secretary of State for Scotland at the time. His successor Michael Forsyth, though equally fallible, would have been more difficult to find a rhyme for. It would be equally difficult to substitute Colin Montgomerie for Sandy Lyall, but less so to substitute Craig Brown for Andy Roxburgh.

Grandad's Birthday

The scene is a nursing home. An old man (Steve) wearing a badge proclaiming, 'I am 95' is wheeled in by his son Andrew (Buff), who parks the wheelchair beside a small table on which there is a telephone.

Andrew. Well, Father, today's the day. Ninety-five today.

Grandad. Aye. An I finished my porridge.

A. I must say the nursing home's doing you proud. Are you looking forward to your special birthday tea?

G. Aye, fairly.

A. So are all the other residents. I just spotted two of your girl friends on the way in. Dressed to kill. Both in their nineties.

G. Baith in their nighties? This is gaan tae be a better pairty than I thocht.

Telephone rings. Andrew picks it up.

A. Hello? No, this isn't Mr William Fraser. This is his son Andrew speaking. Oh, hello, Bessie. No, Dad's fine. I'll hand you over to him. (*To Grandad.*) It's Bessie phoning from Nottingham.

Grandad takes the phone.

G. Hello, Bessie. This is yer faither spikkin. Fit's the weather like in Nottingham? Weel, ye're lucky. It's been a terrible mornin here. Jist nae takkin time tae come doon. An yesterday wis the same. We hinna hid a summer at aa.

A. Thank her for the gloves that she sent.

G. Andrew says to thank you for the gloves you sent him.

A. Not me. You! It's you she sent the gloves to.

G. Andrew says to thank you for the gloves you sent me. They're lovely gloves. And I got yer card an aa. Fit een wis it I got fae you? Wis it the coos in the water or the sheep in the snaa? The coos in the water. Weel, I got exactly the same een fae Chrissie. Except hers wis £1.65 fae Woolies and yours wis £1.95 fae Boots.

A. Tell her you like the gloves.

G. Andrew says I like the gloves. An I div. I div like the gloves. They're lovely gloves. I look forward tae wearin the gloves. No, I never ging oot. But they'll be cosy for sittin in the TV lounge. Oh, yes. I like the TV. My favourite programme? *One Foot in the Grave*. And I like Cilla. I wid fair like tae be in that *Blind Date*. Fit? Ah, weel, my dear, ye can aye get a sting fae a deid bee. Cheerio. Aa the best. (Puts down phone.) Now, that wis Chrissie.

A. No, Dad. That wasn't Chrissie. That was Bessie. (Phone rings.) That could be Chrissie.

Grandad picks up the phone.

G. Hello? Hello, Chrissie. (*To Andrew.*) It's Chrissie. Hello, Chrissie. Yes, this is yer Dad spikkin. Fit's the weather like in Market Harborough? Weel, ye're lucky. It's been a terrible mornin here. Jist nae takkin time tae come doon. An yesterday wis the same. We jist hinna hid a summer at aa.

A. Ask her about Patricia's new baby.

G. Andrew says tae ask ye aboot Patricia's new baby. Has he got a name yet? Pamela? Weel, you tell Pamela that he's my ninth great-grandchild. An I've eighteen grand-children and six o my ain.

A. Seven, Dad. Seven of your own.

G. Seven? Wait a minute, Chrissie, Andrew says seven. Wait till we work this oot. There's Bessie an Chrissie an Douglas an Elsie an Frank an Gladys – aat's jist six. Fit's aat? I missed oot Andrew? Oh, but Andrew disna coont. He bides here in Aiberdeen. I see him aa the time. It's jist the eens that are awaa that coont. 'Cos I never see them. I mean, I hinna seen neen o the rest o ye since yer mither's funeral. Ye're aa sae far awaa. Ye miss oot on seein me. But Andrew's lucky that wye. He can get in tae see me at ony time. (*To Andrew.*) Faa am I spikkin til here, Andrew?

A. It's Chrissie, in Market Harborough.

G. Oh, Chrissie. Chrissie, how's the weather in Market Harborough?

A. You've asked her that already. Just ring off. Say cheerio.

G. Cheerio, Chrissie. Andrew tells me I've tae ring off. (*To Andrew.*) So foo ye daein the day, Andrew? Did ye mind tae bring the new batteries for my hearing aid?

A. Dash! I forgot.

G. Ye're jist hopeless, Andrew. Ye never mind naething that I need ye tae dae for me. And hiv ye brocht yer wife wi ye the day?

A. No. Elizabeth's broken-hearted that she's missing your party.

G. I'll bet.

A. No, she wouldn't have missed it for the world. But this is the day she's to stay at home and pay the window cleaner. So let's get this clear. Who all have you had on the phone today. You've had Bessie and Chrissie while I've been here. Did anybody phone you before I arrived?

G. No. Naebody never phones me. I did hae yer Uncle Bert on fae New Zealand.

A. Oh, Bert was on the go early.

G. No, He wis late. He wis sayin it's tomorrow in New Zealand. Then I hid Elsie on fae Edinburgh. An she brocht her fower grandchildren tae the phone – aat's fower o my great-grandchildren, and they aa sang ower the phone 'Happy Birthday, dear Great-Grandad.'

A. Aw.

G. Fit a helluva racket.

A. And had Elsie any news?

G. No. Naebody's never nae news for me. She wis tellin me aboot her youngest een, Beatrice, her wi the glesses an the lang hair – like hingin mince – she'll never get a man, Beatrice, but she's going on to do further research at Oxford.

A. Ah, yes. She's a very clever girl, Beatrice. But look, if Frank comes on from Lerwick, don't mention Beatrice to him.

G. Oh?

A. Remember, I told you. The Edinburgh lot don't speak to the Lerwick lot – ever since Beatrice went to Oxford the same week that Frank's lassie Fiona began her new job in Soho as a so-called hostess.

G. Weel, Beatrice his deen affa weel at Oxford.

A. Weel, Fiona's done affa weel in Soho.

Phone rings, Andrew answers it.

A. Hello? Oh, hello, Frank. Yes, Dad's fine. I'll pass you over to him. (*Andrew gives the phone to Grandad.*) It's Frank in Lerwick.

G. Hello, Frank. This is yer faither spikkin. Fit's the weather like in Lerwick? Weel, you're lucky. It's been a terrible mornin here. Jist nae takkin time tae ging doon. An yesterday wis the same. We jist hinna hid a summer at aa.

A. Tell Frank you've had a lot of nice cards.

G. Andrew says I've hid a lot o nice cards. But I hiv. I hiv hid a lot o nice cards. I hid een fae you an Dodo. Noo wis yours the coos in the water or the sheep in the snaa? You wis the sheep in the snaa. 20p fae the Church o Scotland Bookshop sale. Oh, lovely cards, but the een I like best is the fat wifie on the beach wi nae claes on. I think it wis fae Beatrice. (*Andrew gestures desperately.*) Wait a minute, Frank, Andrew's wavin at me. I'm surely nae supposed tae spik aboot Beatrice. She must be the een that's on the game in Soho. Frank? God, he's hung up on me. (*He hangs up.*)

A. I'm not surprised he's hung up on you. It's his lassie Fiona who's on the game in Soho. And we're not supposed to know that. We got that from the Edinburgh lot. And they'd got it in confidence from the Nottingham lot. And they'd got it from the Market Harborough lot. I explained all that to you.

G. Weel, ye canna expect me tae mind aa that complicated things. Ye get mixed

243

up at my age. Ye get a bittie dottled at my age. I'm ninety-five, ye ken. It's my birthday the day. Fit wye did ye nae arrange for me tae get a telegram fae the Queen?

A. 'Cos ye're only ninety-five. Ye're not a hundred.

G. Weel, I feel a hunner, some days I feel affa aal.

A. Weel, ye're not affa aal! Ye're only ninety-five.

G. Weel, I should be a hunner. 'Cos my faither an mither – yer aal Grannie an Grandpa Fraser – they coorted for seven years afore they got mairried. I should be a hunner an two.

Phone rings, Grandad picks it up.

G. I'll tak this een. Hello? Oh, hello. Aye, I ken faa I've got. (*To Andrew.*) It's yer loon, Gordon. He's phonin fae Morocco. Fit's the weather like in Morocco? Sunny? Michty, ye must be haein a better summer in Morocco than we're haein in Aiberdeen. Aye, I've got yer Dad here. But yer Mum couldna come. She hid tae bide in for the windae cleaner. Fit's aat? Ha, ha. (*To Andrew.*) Gordon says he never kent his mither's bidie in wis a windae cleaner. Very good, Gordon. Very good. Ye're jist a tonic. Ye're naething like yer aal man at aa. I doot the brains must've skipped a generation. Thanks for phonin, my loon. It wis affa good o ye tae mind yer aal Granda. Cheerio, Gordon, tak care. Cheerio. (*He hangs up leaving Andrew with his hand hovering over the phone.*) Ye wisna wintin tae spik til him, wis ye?

A. Of course I was wanting to speak to him. That's just typical. I never get to do what I want to do. I come in here to see you every day –

G. Nae every day. Ye werna in here last Tuesday.

A. Last Tuesday? That was the day I'd to go to the dentist to get four teeth out.

G. There ye go. Ye've got time tae ging tae the dentist, but ye hinna got time tae come and see yer peer aal faither.

Andrew grabs Grandad by the throat with a view to strangulation.

The coos in the water or the sheep in the snaa: Grandad clearly appreciated both Constable and Farquharson, though the other evidence to be gleaned from this sketch suggests that he would have preferred a Rubens.

The Diet Starts Tomorrow

Voice / Piano

My chol- es- ter- ol count, Has a ten- den- cy to mount Which I'm
told clogs up my art- er- ies, Said my G. P., "It's a di- et for thee,
Bac- on's off, pies is off, prawns is off." He gave me a list, which
seems to con- sist, Of ev- ery- thing I'm fon- dest of, And
when the Doc said, "Di- et!" we prom- ised we would try it But last
night when we sat doon tae wir tea I

rolled my eyes in hor - ror. It wis

had - dock in bat - ter And Black For - est gat - ta Skip

that? No way I wis forced to say, "The di - et starts to -

mor - ra" We say to - day what we

Verse 6 to Coda

said yes - ter - day "The di - et starts to - mor - row."

1,2,4 ,5

3

I wis mor - ra. Let the di - et be - gin and

My cholesterol count
Has a tendency to mount, which I'm told clogs up my arteries
Said my G.P., 'It's a diet for thee –
Bacon's off, pies is off, prawns is off.'
He gave me a list which seems to consist
Of everything I'm fondest of.
But when the doc said, 'Diet!'
I promised I would try it.

But last night when we
Sat doon tae wir tea
I rolled my eyes in horror:
It wis haddock in batter
And Black Forest gatta –
Skip that? No way;
I wis forced to say,
'The diet starts tomorra.'

CHORUS

We say today what we said yesterday,
'The diet starts tomorrow.'

I wis affa near sick
At a weddin last wik
In the village of Auchterturra;
There wis ashets o tatties,
Baith chappit an sauties,
I blame masel,
I said, 'Ach, tae hell!
The diet starts tomorra.'

On Wednesday last
At a Rot'ry repast
It wis Soddom and Gomorrah:
Syrup sponge and salami –
A big double whammy,
As I clarted my bread
With butter I said,
'The diet starts tomorra.'

CHORUS

Let the diet begin, and my next of kin
Will see that I'm no quitter

(They'll see that he's no quitter.)
Lots of fruit I should eat, so tomorrow for sweet
I'll have a banana fritter
(And profiteroles with his fritter.)

At the Flahertys' do
There's rich Irish stew
And the Guinness flows begorrah!
And sweet Irish coffee much thicker than toffee
Sure let's all go
Where the praties grow
The diet starts tomorra.

CHORUS

I've sworn off pud
And other rich food
More in anger than in sorrow,
But when I get an eyeful
Of dairy cream trifle –
When I see one of those, my will-power goes
And the diet starts tomorrow.

Mars and Milky Ways
Are things nowadays
I would not beg, steal or borrow,
But fudge after dinner –
Forgive this poor sinner!
Can't help myself,
From helping myself,
And the diet starts tomorra.

The diet starts –
No more jam tarts
The diet begins –
No crafty gins
The diet starts tomorra.

Chappit Tatties: Prepared no doubt by Sandy Gandhi (see p. 68) and flown over specially from his Calcutta take-away. The culinary high spot of every society wedding in Auchterturra.

Press Conference

P.A. Ladies and gentlemen of the press – the President of the United States. (*Tape: 'Here Comes the Chief'. Enter Councillor Alexander Swick.*)

Swick. Jist a joke, boys. This is nae real politics. This is Monklands District Cooncil, who are our hosts for this month's special meeting of the Convention of Scottish Local Authorities, COSLA. And may I take this opportunity to publicly repute, or should I say refudiate? the vile allegations gaan aboot that COSLA stands for Collection o Skivin Lay-abouts. Now in the absence of the two Edinburgh delegates, Councillors Mark Lazarowicz and Paolo Signorini, who this evening are attending a meeting of the Scottish Heritage Association, it has fell to my lot, in fact the task has came my way, tae welcome aa you media boys tae this press conference for the launchin o COSLA's riposte tae Ian Lang's White Paper on the reorganisation o local government in Scotland – the most shameful document to be seen in Scotland since Duncan Ferguson's list of previous convictions. But now with this document, our alternative blueprint for reform, we move on to the attack. Now this blueprint – it may look white tae you, but it's blue – ye've aa got copies o't. This is Scotland in the next century. So I'm wintin some good questions fae ye the nicht. Faa's first? Yes, sir.

Edinburgh voice. *The Scotsman* here. Are the proposals contained in your document now in the public domain?

Swick. Eh?

Edinburgh voice. Well, I have studied the proposals, and clearly for the administration of this scheme COSLA itself will need some high calibre well-qualified staff. Do you have anybody in mind?

Swick. Yes, we have secured the services of the City of Aberdeen's distinguished former Chief Executive, Mr Donald Macdonald, VC, DSO, RSVP, NBG. Mr Macdonald now lives quietly in Oldmeldrum where he keeps a few hens, sheep and pigs. Indeed he could be the subject of the old song, 'Old Macdonald had a farm, EIEIO.' Except he's nae entitled tae the EIEIO. Right, next question.

Inverness voice. *Inverness Courier*, Councillor. Whatever your new set-up, I hope municipal building standards are going to be better than they were in the past, when you just threw up a lot of concrete rubbish. Can you not learn from other countries?

Swick. Yes, oh, yes. Only last year I myself was in Athens on a free jaunt – study tour – and while there I visited the Parthenon and the Apocalypse. An fit a state some o that buildins is in. There's naething as bad as that in Scotland. Next question?

Fife voice. *Fife Free Press.* Now that there's mair an mair folk on the dole, the new authorities will have a responsibility to cater for all this extra free time and leisure. What plans do you have for leisure facilities?

Swick. Leisure facilities? The answer lies in one word: Flumes. Water chutes, ken? Flumes is the feature of a fun-filled future. Scotland's never had flumes afore. Throughout its long history, this great nation of ours has been flumeless.

Fife voice. Would it no be better providin ice-rinks instead? What if Torvill and Dean came tae Scotland?

Swick. They'll ging doon the flumes like aabody else. Next?

Wild Highland voice. Councillor, I represent Skye.

Swick. Ah, the *Skye Courier*?

Highland voice. No, the Skye Terrier. And we here on the misty isle are well aware that Scotland's biggest growth industry is tourism. And be they Regions or Districts, local authorities have a big responsibility with regard to the quality end of the tourist trade. Would you care to comment?

Swick. Well, here I can only speak for my own authority – the City of Aberdeen. We are proposing a major tourist attraction – topless bathin. It's aa in the blueprint – page 3 – topless bathin on Aiberdeen beach. So, we're gaan tae pit in undersoil heatin at the beach.

Highland voice. Are you saying Aberdeen beach is cold?

Swick. It's caal in the winter. It's freezin in the summer. Weel, last July, there wis a circus on the Queen's Links – polar bear escapes – rins on tae the beach – five minutes later he's aat caal he gies himsel up. Terrible! Next question?

Glasgow voice. *The Herald*, Glasgow. Living as we do in Scotland where natural assets abound, we have to be very concerned about ecology. How high on YOUR agenda do you place ecology?

Swick. 'E cology? Is aat Jordanhill College? Or the Technology College? Or the Art College? There's a hale heap o colleges. Ye'll hae tae be mair specific. I'm sorry.

Glasgow voice. We're no lettin ye aff wi that, Councillor. It's the environment I'm oan aboot. The whole o Scotland is worried aboot nuclear dumpin. The threat of NIREX has not disappeared completely. What are YOUR views on Nirex?

Swick. Nirex? Indispensable. And ye get them fae slot machines now, you know. Big advance. There's a gentleman in a dog collar. Yes, Reverend Sir. Which paper do you represent?

Presbyterian voice. *Life and Work*. The journal of the Church of Scotland.

Swick. *Life and Work*, yes.

Presbyterian voice. As a man of the cloth, I am very concerned about the current phenomenon of outing.

Swick. Outing?

Presbyterian voice. Yes, outing. Following the activities of Peter Tatchell in England, can you foresee an outing taking place in Scotland?

Swick. Ye mean a bus outin? A charabanc outin?

Presbyterian voice. No, no. I'm referring to an outing involving a clergyman.

Swick. Oh, a Sunday School picnic? I like a Sunday School picnic. As lang as there's a crate o export on the bus comin hame. Next question?

Cockney voice. *Times Educational Supplement*.

Swick. *Times Educational Supplement*.

Cockney voice. What are your views on League Tables?

Swick. Weel, we ken faa's nae gaan tae win the League this year, and that's Aiberdeen. The wik afore he wis sacked, Willie Miller drove at 100 mph alang Union Street. It wis the only wye he could get 3 points. Next question.

Doric voice. *Auchterturra Advertiser* incorporatin the *Clatt Clarion* an the *Rhynie Free Press*.

Swick. Aat's an affa big name for an affa wee paper. Foo often div ye come oot?

Doric voice. Once a year.

Swick. Once a year?

Doric voice. Aye, nae every year. Ye're lucky I'm here the day.

Swick. Fit's yer question?

Doric voice. Weel, Auchterturra wid affa like tae be twinned.

Swick. Twinned?

Doric voice. Aye, twinned. Wi some ither place, like Paris, or Rome or San Francisco. An you're maybe the boy tae advise us.

Swick. I canna see Auchterturra bein twinned wi onywye. Your best bet is a suicide pact wi Mintlaw. Next question?

John Cole. John Cole here – formerly of *Newsnight*, pensioned off by the BBC but now earning a lot more as a freelance.

Swick. John Cole? John Cole! Aat's raised the tone a bittie. Yes, Mr Cole.

John Cole. In the formulation of COSLA's alternative plans for the reorganisation of local government in Scotland have you taken into consideration the need to reconcile the constraints imposed by the Block Grant with the perceived deficiencies of the new council tax and the burden of the Public Sector Borrowing Requirement, bearing always in mind the enormity of the current budget deficit.

Swick. Thank you, Mr Cole. An excellent question. Ten oot o ten for the question.

John Cole. What about the answer?

Swick. Sorry, Mr Cole. Nae supplementaries. But may I say, Mr Cole, I've aye been a great fan o yours. Ken fit I like aboot you, Mr Cole? There's naething pit on aboot ye. Ye're nae ashamed o the wye ye spik. You remain true to your roots, Mr Cole, and the whole of the Rhondda Valley must be proud of you.

Duncan Ferguson: Scottish international footballer. A dangerous striker (of other people), and it wasn't just because of his aerial ability that an Aberdeen fan said of him, 'Duncan Ferguson – fit a heider.'

Torvill and Dean: see footnote Vol. 1, p. 201.

Suicide pact wi Mintlaw: this is an unfair slur on Mintlaw which is no worse than the next place. Mind you, the next place is New Pitsligo.

Willie Miller: in the totally unbiased opinion of the authors, the greatest footballer of all time.

John Cole: the acceptable face of Northern Ireland. Oh, that there were a million and a half more like him!

Talking Britain Down

down. Don't say that our Health Ser -vice soon will reach rock Bot - tom - ley .That's

talk - ing Bri - tain down. Don't say that all our mas - ters are po -

li - ti - cal dis - as - ters, and that Par - lia - ment's the fun - niest show in town. Don't

last verse to Coda

say that our dear Prem - i- er's a real dis - as - ter a - rea. That's talk - ing Bri - tain

Coda

down. Don't scoff at Pe - ter Lil - ley. Don't say

Wal - de - grave is si - ly. Don't say that Nor - man La - mont should have

had his head ex - am - ined. Don't say of Nor - man Fow - ler. He's the

origi - nal school boy how - ler. Don't say that Jaws the shark is, more hu -

mane than Ken - neth Clarke is. That's talk - ing Bri - tain down.

Rule Brit - ann - ia, al - though she's run a - ground. We must ne - ver ne - ver ne - ver talk her

down.

Freedom of speech is a guiding star,
True democrats all hail it,
But freedom of speech can go too far,
When it does, we must curtail it;
People have got to understand
Certain comments must be banned.
If you live in this green and pleasant land
Our leaders will frown
If you talk it down . . .

.

Don't say this land that once was great is second-rate today,
That's talking Britain down.
Don't say that our Health Service soon will reach rock Bottom-ley,
That's talking Britain down.
Don't say that all our masters are political disasters
And Parliament's the funniest show in town;
Don't say that our dear Premier's a real disaster area,
That's talking Britain down.

Don't say that our MPs grow rich on large director's fees,
That's talking Britain down.
Don't say that half the Cabinet is wallowing in sleaze,
That's talking Britain down.
Don't say that Jon'than Aitken eats the Ritz's egg and bacon
But never pays his bill or buys a roun;
Don't say that Britain's tottery if it needs a National Lottery,
That's talking Britain down.

Don't say that BBC TV is going down the tube,
That's talking Britain down.
Don't say that *Eldorado* was a catastrophic boob,
That's talking Britain down.
Don't soil the reputation of this noble Corporation,
That once enjoyed a world-wide renown;
Don't say Lord Reith must often be revolving in his coffin,
That's talking Britain down.

Don't say as far as sport's concerned this country's pretty poor,
That's talking Britain down.
Don't ever say that Gazza's not as nice as Bobby Moore,
That's talking Britain down.
Don't pan, as is the fashion, all
That's wrong with the Grand National,
Don't say the Jockey Club should be put down;
Don't say that our race courses

Should be managed by the horses,
That's talking Britain down.

Don't mention the top people whom Miss Whiplash entertains,
That's talking Britain down.
Don't blame the judge or bishop who enjoys being put in chains,
That's talking Britain down.
Please don't expose the surgeon who with very little urgin
Will dress up in a Vivienne Westwood gown;
Don't say that there are vicars who like wearing ladies' knickers,
That's talking Britain down.

Don't say the Royal Family's an anachronism today,
That's talking Britain down.
Don't say that you'd abolish them if you could have your way.
That's talking Britain down.
Don't say Princess Diana is a scheming little planner,
Don't knock the hangers-on around the Crown;
Don't say the House of Windsor should be fed into the mincer,
That's talking Britain down.

Don't say the way the Maastricht Bill was handled was a farce,
That's talking Britain down.
Don't mutter that this Government keeps falling on its – face,
That's talking Britain down.
Don't scoff at Peter Lilley, don't say Waldergrave is silly,
Don't say that Michael Howard is a clown;
Don't pan the peccadillos of the Rifkinds and Portillos,
Don't say that Norman Lamont should have had his heid examined,
Don't say that Norman Fowler is the original schoolboy howler
Don't say there's no-one dumber than that twit John Selwyn Gummer,
Don't say that Jaws the shark is more humane than Kenneth Clarke is,
That's talking Britain down.
Rule Britannia – although it's run aground,
We must never, never, never, talk it down.

Bottomley: A reference to the Secretary of State for Health at the time, Virginia Bottomley, pronounced by some dissatisfied doctors, nurses and patients to rhyme with Cholmondley.

Princess Diana: little known former nursery teacher, carer and keep-fit enthusiast.

The Mascot

Buff. Those of you who saw our last show may recall that it featured the world's first Doric-speaking parrot, whose name was Rover. What we didn't know at the time was that Rover had had a military career: for many years he was the regimental mascot of the Gordon Highlanders, Auchterturra's own regiment now sadly disbanded. But if the regiment itself has gone, the mascot is still going strong. (*Lights up to reveal the parrot (Steve) wearing a Glengarry.*)

Parrot. Aye, aye, fit like? Aye, aye, fit like? Save the Gordons! Save the Gordons!

B.   Regimental mascot, atten-shun! (*Parrot brings feet together on perch.*) Stand at – ease! (*Parrot moves its feet apart.*) Stand easy! (*Parrot slumps.*) Well, the campaign to save the Gordons has failed.

P. I blame mysel. I blame mysel. I wis ower cocky! I wis ower cocky! I wis a cocky wee Gordon an I counted my chickens. I wis a cocky wee Gordon an I counted my chickens.

B. You shouldn't blame yourself. I blame Malcolm Rifkind.

P. I dinna like Rifkind. I dinna like Rifkind. I do not like Rifkind. I'm jealous o Rifkind.

B. Why should you be jealous of Malcolm Rifkind?

P. He's got a bigger beak than me.

B. When you joined the Army you did ten weeks' basic training?

P. I did ten wiks' trainin in a squad o trainee mascots.

B. What did the training consist of?

P. Square bashin, spud bashin, polishin yer beets, cleanin yer brasses, polishin the fleer, cleanin oot the ablutions – aat's a posh name for lavvies.

B. These animals that had to do all these nasty things, were they wild?

P. Weel, they werna affa pleased.

B. And these potential mascots – were they all different kinds of animals?

P. The barrack room was like a menagerie. I'd an elephant in the next bed. An elephant in the next bed.

B. It had been a big bed?

P. Course it wis a big bed. He wis a heavy sleeper. Big bed, big uniform, big aathing. But he didna hae a kitbag.

B. He didn't have a kitbag?

P. He brocht his ain trunk.

B. Was he very noisy?

P. Aye, fit a snorer he wis. An nae jist snorin.

B. Of course elephants trumpet.

P. Aye, we got reveille in the middle o the nicht.

B. So you'd the elephant on one side. What had you on the other side.

P. I'd a moose.

B. A moose? It had been the mascot of the Canadian Army?

P. I dinna ken faar he cam fae, but he fair got through the cheese.

B. Who was in charge of this barrack room? Who was the NCO?

P. The tiger. He'd mair stripes than onybody else.

B. Surely the zebra would have had more stripes than the tiger.

P. But the zebra disappeared.

B. Disappeared out the door?

P. Disappeared doon the tiger's throat! Fit a mess! Ketchup aawye. Gad sake!

B. I'm trying to picture all these animals on their first day on the parade ground.

P. The first day on the parade ground wis a disaster. I blame the Sergeant Major. I blame the Sergeant Major. We got the command, 'Two paces forward march. Two paces forward march.'

B. What happened?

P. We lost the kangaroo. He louped aff the parade ground and through the cook-hoose windae.

B. He went AWOL.

P. He went ower the waa.

B. Did you form any special friendships among your comrades?

P. I got chummy wi a wee dog. A Scottie.

B. This Scottie – was he a regular soldier?

P. No. He wis a Terrier.

B. But he was the only Terrier. All the other animals in the barrack room were regular?

P. I'll say they were regular. You should've seen the mess on the fleer. It wis like the bottom o a parrot's cage.

B. Now, after your basic training, you all got postings?

P. I pit in for the Gordons. I pit in for the Gordons.

B. And you got the Gordons. Was there a lot of competition?

P. It wis atween me an the giraffe.

B. A giraffe applied for the Gordon Highlanders?

P. He'd the neck for onything.

B. Did you like the giraffe?

P. I'd a lot o respect for im. I looked up tae the giraffe. Ye couldna help lookin up til im.

B. But you beat him – you got the job. But now you're out of a job. After how long? How long were you in the Army?

P. I signed on for 22 years. I signed on for 22 years. I signed on for 22 years.

B. So you did 22 years?

P. I did 66 years. Can ye nae coont?

B. And now after 66 years –

P. I've got early retirement.

B. I was reading somewhere they've given you the honorary rank of colonel.

P. Aat's richt, I'm a colonel. I'm a colonel.

B. So you'll have a reasonable pension?

P. My pension's peanuts. My pension's peanuts.

B. Now that you've retired, where do you live?

P. In the Regimental Museum. In the Regimental Museum. Far they keep aa the silver an the trophies an the stuffed animals.

B. Are you going to be stuffed?

P. I'm aye hopin.

B. Where exactly do you live in the Museum?

P. I've got a billet in the officers' canteen. I've got a billet in the officers' canteen.

B. You describe it as a canteen, but is it a mess?

P. Of course it's a mess. Fit d'ye expect wi a bloody parrot fleein aboot the place?

B. Getting back to where we began, have you abandoned the campaign to save the Gordons?

P. No, I hinna gien up. I hinna gien up. I'm gaan doon tae London tae see the Prime Minister.

B. Down to London? Will you go by plane?

P. No, I dinna like fleein. I dinna like fleein.

B. And what will you say to the Prime Minister?

P. I'm gaan tae get him tae change his mind.

B. How can you expect the Prime Minister to do what you tell him?

P. 'Cos I'm a colonel and he's only a Major.

Glengarry: Regimental cap of the Gordon Highlanders, kindly donated to us by their heid bummer, Lt. Gen. Sir Peter Graham, a good chap – but great Gordon Highlanders! it's just struck us – did we ever give him the two complimentary tickets we promised him?

The Fund-Raiser

Buff. As you will know, Aberdeen University is having a big birthday this year, 500 years old and still going strong. So later this year there'll be a big party to which everyone will be invited. The snag is you're expected to contribute to the fund-raising. Not a lot; unless they know you have a lot. Like the aal fairmer chiel you're about to see. He's just been softened up by a dinner at Chanonry Lodge, the house of Principal Maxwell Irvine, and he's about to be given the treatment by the University's professional fund-raiser, Dermot McBlarney.

Dermot (Buff) and the farmer, Mr Cruickshank (Steve), enter, Dermot first, each carrying a glass of brandy. Cruickshank waves in the direction from which they have come.

C.   Thank you, Principal. Tell Mrs Irvine I enjoyed the semolina puddin.

D.   Come away and sit you down, Mr Cruickshank, and let me put you more fully in the picture.

C.   Weel, I wis kinda half-wonderin fit wye I got an invite tae a do like this.

D.   Yes, well I suppose it's not every day the Principal of the University invites you to dinner with the Chairman of I.C.I., the President of Shell, Sir Ian Wood . . .

C.   And the Maharajah of Magadore.

D.   Quite. One of the three richest men in the world.

C.   An did ye notice? He didna touch the roast beef.

D.   Is he vegetarian?

C.   No. He's a cannibal. But they were aa fine lads. Then there's yersel of course. Faar div you fit in? You're the only een wearin a suit fae Slater's.

D.   Well, in its Quincentenary year, I'm the University's professional fund-raiser.

C.   Oh, ye're a professional fund-raiser. Weel, I jist think I'll awaa hame.

D.   No, no. I'm not here to ask you for money. My job is to give you an overall view of the Quincentenary so that you can feel part of this great occasion.

C.   But fit wye me? Fit wye did ye get a haud o me.

D. You came up on our computer as someone worth targetting. You were identified as 'the head of a North East land-owning and farming dynasty with numerous and substantial assets, inherited and acquired.' What the print-out summary says is –

C. This aal bugger's got a bob or twaa. But faa telt the computer aa that? Dam't! Aal Maitland Mackie's been clypin again.

D. And we also know from the computer that you've taken an interest in another prestigious educational establishment.

C. Aat's richt: Auchterturra Primary School. I founded the Cruickshank Essay Prize.

D. That's right. Just after the War. 1946.

C. Aye. An the first year the subject was 'Where lies farming's future – the horse or the tractor?'

D. And what was the subject this year?

C. Exactly the same. If a thing ain't broke don't fix it.

D. But is that still relevant? Is the horse any use these days?

C. Weel, I dinna ken aboot you, but I couldna get a load o dung oot o a tractor.

D. I notice you were sitting next to the Chairman of I.C.I. at dinner. Did you suggest to him that I.C.I. should start producing dung?

C. Weel, they're needin somethin tae mak their shares grow. So, fit's the catch here, Dermot?

D. Oh, no catch. We're just trying to keep ALL our graduates in the picture.

C. Aa the graduates? Foo mony are there?

D. 35,000.

C. 35,000? An they're aa gettin a denner? Aat's a lot o tatties for Mrs Irvine tae peel.

D. Getting back to your biographical data, I was surprised to find that you did an M. A. and not an agriculture degree.

C. Ah, but aat wis the wye ye did it in my day. Aabody did an M.A. first. Ye couldna be a richt doctor or lawyer or meenister or fairmer unless ye did an M.A. first.

D. Very good. But no longer. *Tempora mutantur et nos mutamur.*

C. Oh, ye did French yersel, did ye? Aat wis it, ye see, ye learned a bittie o this an a bittie o that. But maist o aa ye learned foo much ye didna ken. Daein an M.A. gies ye a rare appreciation o how ignorant ye are.

D. I'm an Arts graduate.

C. There ye go, ye see.

D. How long did it take you to get an ordinary M.A.

C. Weel, I wis at the Varsity fae 1930 tae 1945. Eighteen years. I'd an affa job gettin my ordinary Maths.

D. OK. It was a long time anyway. So what would you say you got out of the University?

C. A bloody good time.

D. Aha! The social life. Well, we hope that during the Quincentenary people will be able to renew old acquaintanceships. Are there any of your contemporaries you would like to meet up with again?

C. Weel, there wis a buxom barmaid in the Kirkgate. There wis twaa or three winsome waitresses in the Refectory. A conductress on the bus atween King's and Marischal.

D. I was thinking about other graduates.

C. You think aboot fit you wint, and I'll think aboot fit I wint. Mind you, there wis an affa bonny lassie sat in front o me in yon lecture room in the corner of the quadrangle yonder, far the wind blaas through.

D. That sounds like the Moral Philosophy classroom.

C. That's richt!

D. So you and this girl were moral philosophers?

C. Weel, I wisna a philosopher, an I'm happy tae say she wisna very moral.

D. Ha, ha! She wasn't an ethics girl.

C. No, she was local. Nellie Strachan her name wis. Fae Finzean. Or wis it Nellie Finzean fae Strachan?

D. Good grief! That must be Dame Helen Strachan, Professor of Philosophy at Cambridge, Mistress of Girton.

C. I'm nae surprised she's somebody's mistress. She wis a cracker.

D. I wouldn't have thought she was your type. She would have been a bluestocking.

C. I dinna ken aboot the colour. Ye never saw the colour – she wis that quick at gettin them aff. Happy days.

D. Yes, that's what it's all about. And that's what the Quincentenary is all about – making sure that future generations have the same chance.

C. Aye, aye, here we go. An if they're gaan tae hae the same chance, ye're needin some money. There's nae sic a thing as a free Quincentenary.

D. Well, you're the one who's mentioned the subject of money. I never mentioned it. But if you could see your way to making a contribution – I mean, in the event of a significant benefaction, the University might be disposed to naming some major new development after you. Your name could ring down the centuries. How about the Cruickshank Hall of Residence for Postgraduate Bidie-ins? Or the Cruickshank Library of Donside & Deeside Erotica? Or how about a completely new University concept – the Cruickshank Institute of Geological Finance?

C. Geological Finance?

D. How to get blood out of a stone. Or what about a chair? Could you fund an Agriculture Chair?

C. I micht rise tae a garden seat. In front o the new Cruickshank Institute o Medical Science.

D. Oh, come on. We're needing £20 million for that.

C. Weel, I jist pit a cheque in the post for £20 million. Twaa wiks ago. An I hinna hid a receipt yet. Hiv ye nae heard aboot aat? I sent it tae the Principal.

D. The Principal doesn't keep me informed of every minor detail. So you've given us £20 million already. You know what this means?

C. It means the Principal's wife's wasted a denner on me.

The Kirkgate: the Kirkgate Bar, a pub which played a crucial role in the authors' education. Indeed in the 1950s it was Aberdeen University's sixth faculty after Arts, Science, Medicine, Law and Divinity. Nowadays, of course, the University has lost all its faculties.

King's and Marischal: the two colleges which comprise Aberdeen University. They didn't merge until the late 18th century, and it is often said with pride by Aberdonians that before then there were as many universities in Aberdeen as there were in England. Of course another way of looking at this is that for a few hundred years there were as many scruffy, irresponsible, sponging layabouts in Aberdeen as there were in the whole of England.

Peter Snow

(Tune: 'When I marry Mr Snow' *Carousel*)

When I'm watching Peter Snow,
I find myself wondering – can this be
A creature from an alien galaxee
Romping round the studio?

He's a human dynamo,
On election night, given half a chance,
Like a pterodactyl with St. Vitus dance
Peter Snow will steal the show.

Elections can get (very) serious,
Then on to the set Peter walks,
And it's laughter nation-wide,
'Cos since Eric Morcambe died
He's the funniest man on the box,
Patrick Moore included.

He darts nimbly to and fro,
Firing off statistics with the child-like joy
Of a four-year-old who's got a brand new toy.
But keep watching Peter Snow:
He'll divert you, he'll amuse you,
Don't try to follow him – he'll just confuse you,
Dear old Peter Snow.

Roughly fifty years ago
The Lord in a mischievous moment designed
A creature that was Goofy and Mick Jagger combined,
And they called it Peter Snow.

Wizard of the high tech show,
There you see the state-of-the-art swingometer,
Then across the screen there comes a lightning blur,
Yes, it's Snow – which way did he go?

He's gone to his magic computer;
No sooner has the first result come up,
Than Peter feeds it in, then predicts who's going to win
The Election, the Grand National and the Cup.
And a Song for Europe.
On comes someone we should know –

Is it Paddy Ashdown? Is it Tony Blair?
Well, the viewing millions simply do not care,
All they want is Peter Snow
You can keep your Paxman, keep your Dimbleby
Let's see Peter do himself an injury,
Oops, a fall of Snow!

His excitement threshhold's low;
Every tiny swing is such a big, big deal,
I fear that in the not too distant future we'll
See the last of Peter Snow,
'Cos though he's slim and not too portly
You feel that the men in white coats will shortly
Come for Peter Snow.

Yet of all the TV pundits no man
Matches this abominable Snow-man,
Good old Peter Snow.

Goofy: Older readers will recall Goofy as a Disney character of bizarre appearance, half animal half human.

Mick Jagger: Even older readers will recall Mick Jagger as a dubious character of even more bizarre appearance, half human half animal.

The Way it Was
(Tape: 'My Heart Stood Still')

Gerry Davis (Buff) and Bernard Balfour (Steve) seated in a studio.

G.D. Hello. Welcome once again to *The Way It Was*. I'm Gerry Davis and with me as usual is local historian and Area Sales Manager for Gillette razor blades, Bernard Balfour.

B.B. Good evening.

G.D. And now to business. And this week's subject is Aberdeen's main thoroughfare, Union Street. Presently celebrating its bi-centenary.

B.B. Not only that, it's 200 years old.

G.D. The first thing to be said about Union Street is that it's a very beautiful street.

B.B. Oh, yes. Well, as far as I'm concerned, you can keep Princes Street, Sauchiehall Street, or even the High Street, Mintlaw. They've all got their own individual charm – with the exception of the High Street, Mintlaw, but to my mind Union Street beats the lot.

G.D. Even Princes Street?

B.B. Certainly. There are shops on both sides of Union Street. And to see the sunshine glinting on the silver granite buildings after a shower of April rain, well, as Lewis Grassic Gibbon once unforgettably said –

G.D. Yes?

B.B. I canna mind. But the sum and substance of it was – it takes a bit of beating. Particularly of course when seen through the rose-coloured specs of a young man accompanied by his girl-friend in her pretty frock, as they walked the mat.

G.D. Walked the mat?

B.B. 'Walking the mat' was the expression applied to the heady and exhilaratin pastime of trailin up an doon Union Street. It was a form of promenading. As you know, Gerry, in Paris the boulevardiers promenaded along the Champs Elysées in their morning coats and toppers with their silver-topped canes. Well, in Aberdeen it was exactly the same, except it wis young loons wi plooks from Kittybrewster.

G.D. So you 'walked the mat' with your girl-friend.

B.B. You walked the mat with your girl-friend in her pretty frock whom you'd met at the Monkey House at the corner of Union Terrace there –

G.D. The Monkey House. Now why was it called the Monkey House?

B.B. I suppose because it was the place where folk hung aboot. As monkeys do.

G.D. Of course it was the great meeting place for courting couples.

B.B. Oh, yes. Many's the time I've been stood up at the Monkey House – there I'd be, love's young dream in my blazer and flannels, or if it was a Sunday, my kilt and my open-toed sandals.

G.D. You mentioned shops on both sides of Union Street. Many of them of course have moved to the Bon Accord Centre.

B.B. Don't mention that philistine modern monstrosity to me.

G.D. Well, it keeps the shoppers dry if it's raining.

B.B. Well I preferred the days when you just had your goloshes and an umbrella – a lot cheaper than a shopping centre.

G.D. Then there's the St Nicholas Centre as well.

B.B. Is that so? I did wonder where Raggie Morrison's had gone. And the 50/- Tailor. And the Rubber Shop.

G.D. The Rubber Shop. That name would have different connotations today.

B.B. Now, Gerry. This is a family programme. You're not on *Living and Growing* now.

G.D. Anyway, there you were, walking the mat, and then – off to the pictures, maybe, with your girl-friend.

B.B. With your girl-friend in her pretty frock. Off to see the latest Tarzan or Abbot & Costello at the Picture House. You'd slip in, the pair of you, into the back row of the 1/9s –

G.D. And that was called 'Going to the flicks'.

B.B. No, it was called 'necking' in those days.

G.D. Necking?

B.B. Just a bit of gentle osculation. I don't know what you would call it today. You see, there was no sex in those days. Sex didn't come along till 1963. Occasionally you would disengage from your necking and look at the screen, and there you'd catch a glimpse of the latest piece of romantic whimsy starring Robert Taylor, Tyrone Power –

G.D. Ah! They were the De Niros and Pacinos of those days.

B.B. No. The De Niros had the ice-cream shoppie in Windmill Brae, just behind the Picture House. And the Pacino's had the Kit Kat.

G.D. Where, after the pictures, you'd go with your girl-friend –

B.B. In her pretty frock.

G.D. In her pretty frock, for a Knickerbocker Glory.

B.B. That was the nearest you got to knickers in those days. And there was never any question of glory. 'Cos this was long before 1963.

G.D. You mentioned 'walking the mat'. What was that like? Can you give us an action replay? Take us through it, starting at the Castlegate.

B.B. Starting at the Castlegate the first thing you come to is the Town House. Not much activity there. Some things don't change. Then we're at E&M's. And there in the doorway – a few Celtic supporters lingering, doing as Celtic supporters do in E&M's doorway. So it's as well we've on wir goloshes.

G.D. Then we get to the top of St Nicholas Street.

B.B. Where Queen Victoria used to stand. Then she moved to Queen's Cross. That's the peculiar thing about Aberdeen's statues. They move about. You don't get that kind of thing with Nelson's Column. I mean, as for the Duke of Gordon –

G.D. Now in Golden Square.

B.B. Yes, but there was a while he didn't know if he was coming or going.

G.D. Well, leaving Queen Victoria we move on to the Queen's Cinema.

B.B. Named after Queen Victoria. She used to meet Prince Albert there. He would nip down off his pedestal in Union Terrace, and scurry round to see her.

G.D. The Queen's Cinema is now Eagles Night Club. And of course further up there's Zig Zag and the Cotton Club. That's the scene in the 1990s. What was the equivalent in the old days? What did you do for night life?

B.B. We just went to wir bed early.

G.D. Nowadays, of course, people are very security-conscious: concealed cameras, at various points in Union Street. Was there any equivalent in the old days?

B.B. Well, there was just the old night-watchie, sitting in his huttie warming his hands at the brassiere.

G.D. Brazier.

B.B. It depended which night-watchie was on duty.

G.D. On we go, past King Edward VII.

B.B. And there's a pigeon, sh–sh–sheltering under his orb and sceptre. Very painful.

G.D. Continuing further up, we come to a major landmark, the Music Hall.

B.B. Scene of many spectacular civic occasions, freedom ceremonies and the like. I remember being at one where we were addressed by a heroic figure, the great man who had led us to Victory in Europe.

G.D. Winston Churchill?

B.B. Alex Ferguson.

G.D. Anyway, we're getting near the top of Union Street now.

B.B. That's right. Babby Law as it was called in the old days. And of course in those days there was a split-the-wind there. One road took you along Holburn Street to the Bridge of Dee and then Stonehaven; the other one on to Queen's Road, Hazlehead, out the Skene Road and eventually all the way to Alford.

G.D. Well, that's still the case.

B.B. I didn't say it wasn't!

G.D. And when you and your girl-friend reached the split-the-winds –

B.B. Her in her pretty frock, me in my kilt and sandals –

G.D. Which road did you take?

B.B. It didna maitter – she never let me get very far.

The Way it Was: This popular Grampian Television programme featured Gerry Davis as presenter, Bernard Balfour as resident expert and many, many miles of flickering cine footage.

Lewis Grassic Gibbon: aka Leslie Mitchell, commentator on British Movietone News, a prime example of the aforementioned flickering cine footage.

Retirement

Alec (Steve) and Norman (Buff) are discovered at one side of the stage. Alec wears a smart straw hat, Norman a white bunnet. Alec mimes the delivery of a bowl, then runs after it.

A. Ach! I'm ower thin.

N. Aye, ye're ower thin, Alec.

A. I'm ower thin. Copie milk. But I'm still lyin the shot, Norman. An ye're blocked on baith hands. Ye hinna a hope.

N. Weel, there's only one thing for it, Alec. I'll hae tae drive.

A. Drive? Watch yersel, Norman. Ye hinna played a drive since ye hid yer second hip replacement.

N. Weel, but needs must. I'll jist hae tae go for it.

A. Weel, it's up tae yersel, Norman. Hiv ye ony last message for Tibby?

N.   Stand back, Alec. (*He plays.*)

A.   God, ye're nae up, Norman. I've never seen that afore. Playin a drive an nae bein up. Ye're something special. I bet David Bryant's never played a shot like aat.

N.   Weel, it's fair connached me. I think we deserve a seat, Alec. Jist for five meenits.

A.   God, we've only been PLAYIN for five meenits. The score's 1-1.

N.   I'm nae carin. I'm needin a seat. (*They sit.*) Aye, it's a young man's game, the bools. I widna care, fan I wis a loon I thocht it wis jist aal mannies that played bools.

A.   An noo it's a game for young loons. I blame the TV.

N.   Aye, television's a lot tae answer for.

A.   Aat's richt. An there's ower much sex an violence an aa.

N.   On the bowlin green? Faar aboot?

A.   No, no! So – how are ye enjoyin yer retirement, Norman?

N.   Nae a lot. There's nae enough tae dae, Alec. The time jist drags.

A.   Weel, it's a big change for ye, Norman.

N.   Aat's richt, I mean, fan ye've worked flat oot aa yer days weel, ye ken fit I wis like fan I wis workin.

A.   Oh, I ken fit ye mean. Ye wis jist a human dynamo. A coiled spring.

N.   Weel, aat's richt. An ye see, it's nae easy for somebody like me tae slow doon.

A.   Nae easy? It's impossible for you tae slow doon. If ye went ony slower ye'd be gaan backwards.

N.   Weel, I'll tell ye this. Since I retired I find time hings heavy on my hands.

A.   Aye. An foo lang's that ye've been retired, Norman?

N.   Three days.

A. Three days? I didna ken it wis as lang as that.

N. Aye, it's three days. Monday wis aa richt. I wis still unwindin efter the excitement o my presentation. But on Tuesday the hale day I jist sat aboot the hoose, thinkin.

A. Oh, ye wis thinkin! Weel, ye never did that fan ye worked for the cooncil.

N. Then aboot six o'clock I got my tea. Then I sat doon in front o the TV an fell asleep.

A. Ye'd been watchin Grampian, wis ye?

N. Next thing I kent, Tibby wis shakkin me by the shooder an sayin, 'Waaken up, Norman, it's time tae ging tae yer bed.' I mean, is aat it, Alec? Is this fit retirement's gaan tae be like the hale time?

A. No, no. But it's up tae yersel. Ye see, it's twaa years past the 6th o June that I retired, an I've never been sae busy.

N. Is aat richt, Alec?

A. Never been sae busy. An you could be the same. Ye could learn new skills.

N. Weel, Tibby is teachin me the wye tae work the microwave.

A. There ye are, ye see.

N. Aye, fan we got it five years ago, I says tae Tibby, 'Fan I retire I'll hae time tae learn tae work aat thing.'

A. Aat's richt, aat's richt.

N. But ye see, anither twaa months an I reckon I'll hae it licked, an then fit'll I dee?

A. Ye could learn tae pre-set the video.

N. There's nae need tae be sarcastic, Alec. I mean, fit div you find tae dae wi yersel?

A. Weel, I've never been sae busy.

N. But fit exactly div ye DAE?

A. Weel, I've got my dish-washer tae see til. I stack the plates efter breakfast and if there's been a fried egg, I've tae wash the plates afore I pit them in, and wash them again efter I tak them oot. It taks a lot longer than washin the dishes by hand. Then I pit oot my bucket on a Monday and a Thursday, an I tak it in on a Tuesday an a Friday. An there ye go – it's Setterday afore ye ken far ye are.

N. Michty, Alec, there must be mair tae life than pittin oot an takkin in the bucket.

A. Of course there is. God! There's never a wik gings past but I've a funeral tae ging til. If I'm lucky there's twaa.

N. Oh, weel, aat's nae sae bad. I canna be deein wi weddins but I dinna mind a good funeral.

A. Weel, ye can start the morn. 'Cos ye heard aboot Archie Walker?

N. No.

A. Drapped doon deid in the middle o his yalla pea soup.

N. Oh, that's terrible, that.

A. Aye, peer Archie.

N. Terrible. Yalla pea soup's my favourite.

A. But it's a great wye tae go, Norman. Half-wye through a plate o second day's yalla pea soup.

N. Second day's! An he wis only half-wye through't? Oh, aat wis hard luck, aat.

A. Hud on! Aat could mean his wife pit the rest o't back in the pot. Wi a bit o luck we'll maybe get it efter the funeral.

N. So ye've never been sae busy, div ye say?

A. Never been sae busy, Norman.

N. Fit's the best day o the wik?

A. Thursday, Norman.

N. Fit wye's aat?

A. Aat's the day ye get yer pension.

N. Foo much will I get?

A. Weel, it aa depends on yer circumstances, Norman. There's a rebate here, a reimbursement there, here a concession, there an allowance, a bittie taen aff there, a bittie added on here, an Tibby comes intil't an aa, there's a suppie benefit an a bittie supplement, tak awaa the number ye first thocht o an Bob's yer uncle – that is your senior citizen's entitlement.

N. Sounds far ower complicated for aal folk tae understand.

A. Of course it is. That's the hale idea. If the aal folk got aathing they were entitled til, there wid be naething left for the boss o British Gas. But you ask Beldie Gatt at the Post Office fit ye're entitled til. She'll keep ye richt.

N. I widna wint Beldie Gatt tae fin oot aboot my confidential affairs.

A. Oh, she winna fin oot. She kens it aa already. So – fit did ye get for yer presentation, Norman.

N. I got a camcorder.

A. A camcorder? Ye mean I'm playin bools wi the Steven Spielberg o Auchterturra?

N. I dinna ken aboot aat, but afore I cam oot here this mornin I made a tape o Tibby daein the hooverin an makin the bed, and then she took me clippin the hairy bits o my lugs. An efter wir tea the nicht we'll sit doon an watch it.

A. Oh! Fit a nicht that'll be. An ye're complainin ye've naething excitin tae dae!

N. An I'll be takkin the camcorder on wir big trip an aa.

A. Oh, ye're gaan on a big trip, are ye?

N. Aye, we're gaan oot tae visit a cousin in Toronto.

A. Are ye gaan wi SAGA?

N. No, I'm gaan wi Tibby. I dinna wint til, but it's her cousin.

A. It is a male cousin or a female cousin?

N. Female. Maggie Jane. She went oot tae Canada fan she wis a lassie o twinty-three.

A. Foo aal is she noo?

N. Ninety-three.

A. Oh, ye'll hae a lot tae spik aboot, Norman. Ye'll hae a lot tae catch up on. Hiv ye kept up wi her?

N. Jist a Christmas caird.

A. Jist a Christmas caird?

N. Aye, aboot 1943, I think it wis.

A. But aat'll be a great trip, Norman. Fan are ye gaan?

N. July 1997. An I canna wait for it tae come.

A. Norman, dinna wish yer life awaa min.

N. Weel, there's naething tae dae here.

A. Of course there is. I've never been sae busy. I dinna ken fit tae dae first.

N. Fit DIV ye dae first? Tak us through yer day.

A. Weel, ilka mornin at 8 o'clock I ging for the paper.

N. We get oor paper delivered.

A. Fit div ye get yer paper delivered for?

N. Tae save time.

A. Save time? Ye've ony amount o time. Ye're complainin ye've ower muckle time. Ye're tryin tae fill in time. An if ye're tryin tae fill in time, savin time's a waste o time.

N. Weel, I suppose I could ging tae the paper shop. It's only five minutes' walk if I tak the short cut.

A. Weel, dinna tak the short cut! Ging the lang wye roon. It's good exercise. Better for ye. Ye'll live langer.

N. Fit div I wint tae live langer for? There's naething for me tae dae.

A. Give me strength! Weel, but we're gettin there, Norman. Ye see, efter ye ging for yer paper – the lang wye roon – ye ging for yer milk.

N. We get oor milk delivered.

A. Cancel the bloody milk.

N. Wait a minute. I've tae ging for the milk an ging for the paper.

A. Aat's richt. Ging for yer milk and ging for yer paper. Then ging tae the doctor for yer prescription.

N. Fit wid I ging tae the doctor for a prescription for? There's naethin wrang wi me!

A. Aat disna metter. Aabody that's retired gings tae the doctor for a prescription.

N. But if there's naethin wrang wi me?

A. Weel, it's up tae the doctor tae find something wrang wi ye. Surely ye've got a sair back, hivn't ye? Like aabody else?

N. Some days I hiv. In the mornin efter I get up. Ither days it's nae till the efterneen.

A. Oh, some days ye dinna get a sair back till the efterneen?

N. No, some days I dinna get up till the efterneen.

A. Fit else can we get for ye tae dae? Weel, ye can see tae aa yer personal affairs. I mean, lookin tae the future, Norman, hiv ye made yer will?

N. Aye.

A. I suppose aathing'll ging tae Tibby.

N. No. I'm nae leavin naething tae Tibby.

A. Oh, Fit wye nae?

N. She's got it aa already.

A. Noo, fit else? Fit else? I ken – hiv you an Tibby bocht yer plot yet?

N. Fit wid I wint a plot for? I dinna like the gairden I've got.

A. Nae that kind o plot. Hiv ye bocht yer lair at the cemetery?

N. No, I hinna. Tibby says she jist wints tae ging in aside her mither. So I says, 'Weel, if you ging aside yer mither I'm nae comin wi ye.'

A. Norman, ye widna hae tae spik til er. Onywye, ye widna be aside er. If Tibby gings first, you will be on tap o her.

N. God, aat taks me back. First time for thirty years.

A. Mind you, the chances are you'll ging first, and then Tibby wid be on tap o you.

N. First time ever.

A. Norman, I'm daein my best, but ye're jist nae tryin tae help yersel! Noo, this is an offer I widna mak tae onybody: wid ye like tae jine oor coffee school?

N. You've aye telt me there wis nae room in your coffee school.

A. Weel, but there's a vacancy noo, thanks tae half a plate o yalla pea soup.

N. I dinna think a coffee school wid be my cup o tea. Fit happens in a coffee school onywye?

A. Weel, ye hae a cup o coffee, an ye set the world tae rights, spik aboot the fitba, spik aboot the politics, tell the ither lads fit ye've been daein –

N. Weel, I keep tellin ye, I've naething tae dae, so I widna hae naething tae tell them. Fit div ye say if ye've naething tae tell them? I mean, fit'll you be tellin them the morn?

A. Fit'll I tell them the morn? I'll tell ye fit I'll tell them. I'll tell them never tae hae a game o bools wi a miserable aal bugger like you.

Second day's yalla pea soup: 'One of the great dishes of the world.' Escoffier. 'Gings roon yer hert like a hairy worm.' Ena Baxter.

We Are Failing
(Tune: Sailing)

Buff. So this is farewell. Why are we retiring? Well, we got the message earlier this year when we went to see Rod Stewart at Pittodrie.

All. We felt dodd'ry
At Pittodrie
B. See'n' Rod Stewart's energy,
S. But we reckon
By the end he wis pechin,
G. But if he's failin, so are we.

All. We are failing
We are failing
So this show is our farewell.
G. On we stagger,
B. A bittie gaga –
S. Aal age disna come itsel.

All. We're a hat trick
Of geriat-trics
And we're smoarin wi catarrh.
G. We are creakin,
S. Metaphoric'lly speakin –
B. It's nae metaphor – we really are.

All. Aye we're creakin,
Oor joints are squeakin,
We can mind when we were swack.
S. We were slimmer,
B. We were trimmer,
G. Noo my zimmer's parked oot the back.

G. Nae too swack now,
S. Dodgy back now,
B. It's a job jist takin a bow,
G. Antiquated,
S. Dilapidated
B. Superannuated
All. As of now.

G. Fit's the Doric
S. For prehistoric?

B.   'Cos we date back to afore BC.
         We've lost wir energy,
S.   We've baith hid surgery.
G.   They're nae the men they used tae be.

All. Three Methuselahs,
         These days we're useless –
         Nae fit every woman wants.
G.   We're gey crumbly,
B.   Gettin fumbly,
S.   We keep scalin aa doon wir fronts.

All. We keep scalin
         Because we're failin,
         It's time tae end these schoolboy games.
         We have traivelled,
         But noo we're raivelled,
         Canna mind each ither's names.

         So we're retiring.

Fittie Folk

CHORUS

> Fittie folk, Kitty folk, country folk and city folk,
> Folk fae Constitution Street and folk fae Rubislaw Den.
> Wallfield, Nellfield, Mannofield and Cattofield,
> Lots o local stories that ye maybe dinna ken.

VERSE

G. I mind last season fan the Dons hid sic a nerra shave.
B. If aal Dick Donald hid been alive he'd've been turnin in his grave.
S. I mind fan Donald McDonald's false degrees made aabody fizz.
All. We widna mind a golden handshake half the size o his.

B. I mind fan every hoose pit oot its bucket, rain or shine.
S. Noo we've got black bags instead, which suits the seagulls fine.
G. I mind the Gorbachev freedom lunch – a waitress nearly dee'd.
B. She tried tae wipe fit she thocht wis raspberry jeely aff his heid.

S. I mind the height o the ile fan Provost Collie ruled the scene.
G. A Yank enquired, 'Is this the biggest man in Aiberdeen?'
B. I mind fan the University wis founded years ago,
All. In 1495 – the year we met in the Student Show.

G. . . . But now it's time to say . . .

FINAL CHORUS

All. Thanks tae the Fittie folk, country folk an city folk,
Folk that laughed a lot an folk that didna laugh at aa;
Smert folk, shabby folk, back-'n'-fore-tae-the-lavvy-folk –
You've been really great, but noo it's time we were awaa.

Student Show: Nursery for eager hopefuls, some of whom, without ever becoming the new kids on the block, eventually became the old blokes on the skids.

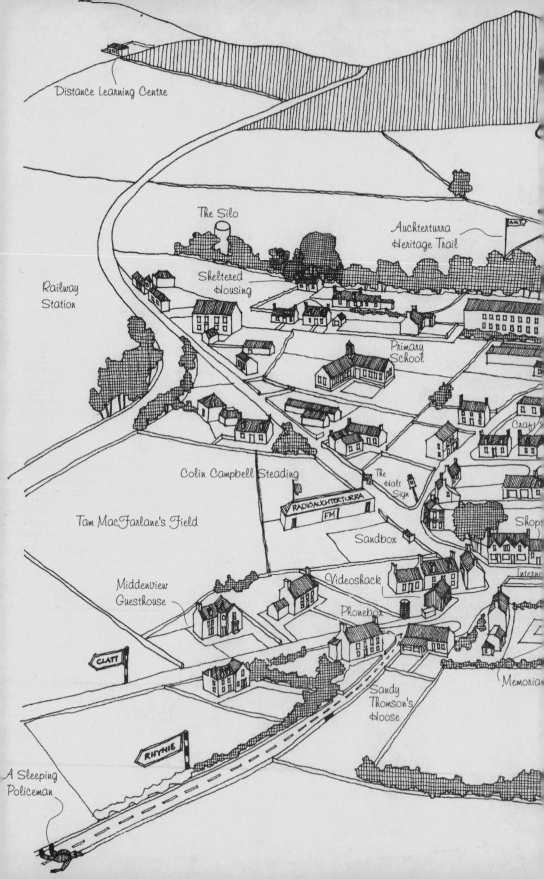

Distance Learning Centre

The Silo

Auchterturra
Heritage Trail

A.H.T.

Railway
Station

Sheltered
Housing

Primary
School

Craft's

Colin Campbell Steading

The
Halt
Sign

Tam MacFarlane's Field

RADIO AUCHTERTURRA
FM

Sandbox

Shops

Internet

Videoshack

Middenview
Guesthouse

Phonebox

CLATT

Sandy
Thomson's
Hoose

Memoria

RHYNIE

A Sleeping
Policeman